Early Praise for

Believe Deeper

"*Believe Deeper* is an invitation to reflect deeply, respond authentically, and be transformed by God. Laura gently leads the reader to go beyond head knowledge and allow God to do His deep work in the spaces that are 'under the waterline of awareness.' She wonderfully weaves together deep biblical truth with honest glimpses of how those truths have transformed her, and then calls us to join in."

—Shanthini Baskaran, PhD, Soul Care Institute

"Laura's honesty and humor are hard to resist as you unearth what's beneath the surface of your thoughts, behaviors, and actions. As a participant in Laura's discipleship group, I have experienced the tenets that are so eloquently shared in *Believe Deeper*. This journal invites you to sit in the hard places, pay attention to what's behind your actions and emotions, and step into the true freedom God has for you when you see Him and how He sees you more clearly."

—Casey Hushon, Executive Director, Hope Church

"There is no greater pursuit than knowing God. Do you agree? Do you want to experience the freedom Jesus gives 'down into your bones'? Then you need to read this book! Laura will uncover the many ways we deceive ourselves into thinking we already know everything about God . . . and ourselves. She uses humor, real-people examples, surprising vulnerability, heartfelt teaching, and wise discipleship to show us. Once you've slowly worked your way through this book, you will *Believe Deeper*."

—Cindy McMartin, Ministry Care Coordinator, Fort Wilderness

"Many of us skim across the surface living unexamined lives. After all, who really has time for self-reflection? And aren't we supposed to focus on others rather than on ourselves? Moreover, what if I uncover stuff I really don't like? In *Believe Deeper*, Laura not only outlines why getting under the surface of our lives is essential to our spiritual formation, but she also leads us through the excavative work that is necessary to live a deeply formed life that is attentive to God's transformative work. If you want to go deeper with Jesus, work through this response journal slowly and prayerfully. I'm confident as you dig deep below the surface, you'll discover the God who is perfect love waiting for you with arms wide open."

—Mac McCarthy, Lead Pastor, Crosspoint Community Church

BELIEVE
DEEPER

12-week response journal

To Expose Doubt and
Transform Faith

Laura E. Sandretti

www.ten16press.com - Waukesha, WI

For Patricia,

Thank you for walking ahead of me in discipleship and for giving me time, vision, and grace in the hard parts of that journey (and for teaching me to give those things to myself, as well). Thank you for reminding me, when I wanted to quit, that every difficult season would be worth the struggle. And thank you for helping me *experience* the freedom Christ died to give me in my actual life. I love you, sister.

Your Cactus-Hugging Friend,
Laura

TABLE OF CONTENTS

Introduction

"Nearly all wisdom we possess, that is to say, true and sound wisdom, consists in two parts: the knowledge of God and of ourselves . . . There is no deep knowing of God without a deep knowing of self and no deep knowing of self without a deep knowing of God."
John Calvin

Four years ago, I participated in an awful discipleship group.

I told the facilitator that every time I came to one of our weekly meetings, I felt like a contestant on the show *Naked and Afraid*. I felt exposed sharing with other women the deep, dark, ugly places in my heart and mind that I had not spent much time thinking about before. It was embarrassing to admit that I was not experiencing joy or peace in most areas of my life, especially since I had been a Christian for so long. I felt vulnerable realizing I still had so many doubts and questions about the Lord and my faith that I thought was solid and unwavering.

Believe Deeper is a glimpse into what I learned in that discipleship journey. Jesus did not disciple people using a book or response journal. He consistently and simultaneously loved and challenged His followers face-to-face, the only way to go and make disciples.

However, what I learned that year, in my naked and afraid-ness, did something to my soul. That challenging group ignited something in me by beginning to remove the scales of my doubt and disbelief from my eyes, scales I did not know existed. Before we can see more clearly, we have to come to the realization that our vision is obscured in the first place. We need to discover how to do that which Calvin attributed as true and sound wisdom, a deeper knowing of God and a deeper knowing of self. I pray this book will help you reflect and respond in a way that moves you to a deeper knowing of both.

Ninety Percent

I recently saw an article entitled "Why Your Mind Is Like an Ice-berg," affirming what Freud deduced over a hundred years ago. Akin to a mostly concealed, dangerous chunk of sea ice, neuroscientists agree that the hidden, subconscious part of our brain makes up at least *ninety* percent of our total brain function. The article also said that this ninety percent is "a vast collection of unintentional, habitual thoughts, behaviors, and actions,"[1] and although those thoughts, behaviors, and actions are difficult to change, they impact our lives significantly every day.

Scripture, of course, confirmed long before Freud that most of the thoughts that control what we say and do are hidden deep within us. It was Jesus who said, "What comes out of a man is what makes him 'unclean.' For from within, out of men's hearts, come evil thoughts, sexual immorality, theft, murder, adultery, greed, malice, deceit, lewdness, envy, slander, arrogance, and folly" (Mark 7:20b-22). Luke 6:45 says that it is our heart that motivates and informs what we say and do. Scripture also acknowledges that our heart is "deceitful above all things and beyond cure" (Jeremiah 17:9a). In Psalms 139:23-24, David alludes to the inseparable union and work-

---

[1] (John, 2014)

ings of the heart and mind: "Search me, O God, and know my heart; test me and know my anxious thoughts."

Theologian George Eldon Ladd said that the most important word Paul used to characterize the human being was the Greek word for the heart, *kardia*[2] (517), and one of the ways *kardia* was used in the New Testament was for human intellectual activity. "In Romans 1:21, the heart of ungodly people is without understanding. In 2 Corinthians 9:7, Paul exhorts his reader to give liberally, 'as he has made up his mind [*kardia*]' (RSV). The 'eyes of the heart' must be enlightened (Ephesians 1:18) to understand the Christians' hope"[3] (518). In this vein, it is the author of Hebrews that reminds us that it is God's Word that helps discern and enlighten the eyes of our heart (Hebrews 4:12).

What does paying attention to the unintentional thoughts, behaviors, and actions hidden deeply in the ninety percent of our intellectual *kardia* have to do with knowing God and ourselves better, and how does it help us believe deeper? Luther said, "Nothing can take away sin except the grace of God. In *actual living*, however, it is not so easy to persuade oneself that by grace alone, in opposition to every other means, we obtain the forgiveness of our sins and peace with God"[4] (italics added, 13). What I've learned about paying attention to what goes on in my heart and mind without my awareness is that when those hidden things are inconsistent with how I feel and how I respond in my actual living, it often exposes doubts I have about God. When I become aware of struggles in my conversations, relationships, and emotions, I can see more clearly that many of my beliefs about the Lord don't impact my real life. Perhaps an embarrassing personal example will illustrate this disconnect.

I was taken aback when the woman whisked back the sporty pink goggles she was wearing when she stopped at the bottom of the ski

---

[2] (Ladd, 1993)
[3] (Ladd, 1993)
[4] (Luther, 2011)

hill. She had a flawless completion, impeccably applied makeup, and a beautiful smile. The commentators for the freestyle Olympic skiing event confirmed my observation. Eileen Gu was not only an Olympiad, but also a professional model. After Ms. Gu soared in almost superhuman fashion on her next jump, the commentators remarked that she had also earned a 1580 on her SATs and was an exemplary pianist. When the seemingly perfect Eileen Gu went on to win the gold medal, I rolled my eyes and thought, "How about saving some of your amazingness for the rest of us, Eileen?"

If you asked me to tell you what I believe about Jesus, I would tell you that I love Him and I know He loves me. I believe it so deeply that I teach women in my speaking and writing ministry that they are fearfully and wonderfully made (Psalms 139:14) and that they are delighted in and rejoiced over with singing (Zephaniah 3:17). I remind my children and friends that their worth and identity are not contingent on what they do or look like because the Lord looks at the heart (1 Samuel 16:7). However, in my actual living, I'm a fifty-two-year-old woman who's threatened and annoyed by an eighteen-year-old freestyle skier. Under the waterline of my own awareness, while I was eating Fritos in my sweatpants and watching the Olympics, I was feeling judgmental and jealous. Paying attention to my unintentional thoughts revealed a disconnect between what I believed deeply for others and what I believed for myself. A disconnect I would otherwise have missed.

Many of us know Romans 8:11 says that the same Spirit that raised Jesus from the dead lives inside us, but based on that eye twitch we have about whether or not we'll get that work project done on time, we wonder if what's inside us is on strike or taking a nap. Some of us have memorized 2 Timothy 1:7, "For God has not given us a spirit of fear, but of power and of love and of a sound mind" (NKJV), but our daughter's new boyfriend keeps us awake at night. I *know* the Bible says God works all things together for good (Romans 8:28) and that His strength is made perfect in weakness (2 Corinthians 12:9). However, if in my actual living I'm struggling to quit yelling at my children, manipulating people, and being jealous of Eileen Gu, there is a significant disconnect between what I believe abstractly and the core beliefs in my actual life and living.

Tim Keller said of the hundreds of pastoral letters written by the famous English pastor and abolitionist John Newton, "Decades of constantly reading and re-reading the [Newton] letters have taught me how to do better analysis of underlying motives, so that when the high doctrines of grace are preached and applied, they do not merely press on the will but change the heart."[5] Faith in Jesus Christ that never threatens, improves, or impacts our job, marriage, and free time does not change the heart. A deeper knowing of how Jesus Christ intersects or fails to intersect with how we respond in our actual relationships and struggles helps us begin to unearth the doubts about our faith that make it feel stagnant and meaningless. Paying attention to the disconnects revealed by our "unintentional thinking, habits, and actions," that is, our ninety percent, can help us identify when grace is pressing on the will as opposed to changing our heart.

Grace that presses on the will feels forced and leaves you fatigued. It makes you question if your faith is doing much in your actual life despite how hard you are trying. Grace that changes the heart, however, feels safe and serene. Theologian Matthew Henry said, "Grace is the free, undeserved goodness and favor of God to mankind." Grace, by definition and because of the cross of Christ, can only be received. *Believe Deeper* will help you unearth and examine your ninety percent, and in doing so, you will move closer to grace that changes the heart. This soul-level, but subtle change will feel like your faith is doing something in your actual living, something not caused by trying harder, but by simply surrendering to Christ's love and acceptance over and over again. And that something feels like freedom.

---

[5] (Reinke, 2015)

Caveats and Cautions

"I don't know where to start, and I don't understand what I'm reading."

That's what my friend said to me after I asked her what she had been reading lately in God's Word. When I asked if she had told the Lord that she didn't know where to start and didn't understand the Bible, she rolled her eyes and chuckled at my rhetorical question. Although this book, by the power of the Holy Spirit, may help you realize some disconnects between knowing *about* faith and experiencing it in your actual life, it will not do anything without you first spending time in your Bible. If the thought of reading God's Word seems difficult or like an obligation, tell that to the Lord. Ask Him for help in giving you the desire to read His Word, but meanwhile, don't stop reading *while* you pray.

Years ago, I began asking the Lord to give me the desire to read His Word, because up until then, I only read it because I knew "good Christians" were supposed to read their Bible. In the meantime, though I didn't particularly feel like it, I continued reading God's Word. Slowly and seemingly imperceptibly as I prayed and continued in Scripture, God helped and continues to help me *want* to stay connected to Him through His Word. Because our feelings about reading the Bible and what we are reading in the Bible can wax and wane, continuing to read it when you don't feel like it is for *you*, not God. Consistently hiding His Word in my heart whether I felt like it or not has given me His supernatural peace, perspective, and hope when I've needed it most and could not see or feel any of those feelings by any other means. I cannot tell you the number of times the rug was pulled out from under me, and the only thing that gave me a shred of hope was His Word, hidden deeply in my heart.

Another consideration before reading this book is that most of us assume we already know what we think and believe about ourselves and God, and in part, we do. However, as we practice looking below the surface of our thoughts and actions, it will be advantageous to ask the Lord to help us keep open minds. Just this week, a woman who has been in the discipleship group I've been facilitating every week for the last seven months confessed something to me. She said that although I have frequently talked about the condemning voice often subtly playing under the waterline of our own awareness, she did not think that was true for her. However, within the last two weeks, she realized, in her ninety percent, that there's an almost constant narrative running in the background of her mind, condemning almost everything she does and says. Asking the Spirit to widen the lens of our imagination for the "more" He has for us will help us recognize things that chip away at our identity, worth, and freedom in Christ, things we are usually blind to.

Although freedom and deeper belief sound good and we welcome them abstractly, exposing our unintentional, habitual thoughts, behaviors, and actions in our actual lives can make us feel naked and afraid. Remember to continually ask the Lord for strength while you read and respond to His invitation to more. Ask Him to help you trust deeply and concretely that His power is made perfect when we're at our weakest, even if you do not feel it. The Spirit will not abandon us as we traverse into deep and unfamiliar territory.

Tell Me What to Do

There is one thing women usually say when they begin to expose disconnects between what they thought they believed deeply and their actual living: "Tell me what to do." Our human nature makes us want to avoid suffering and quickly fix whatever ails us, but sadly nothing about learning to pay attention to the deep, dark lies and partial beliefs in our ninety percent is quick or painless. If a book, facilitator, or Google could simply tell us what to do, none of us would be struggling with why our faith isn't impacting our lives in the way we hoped in the first place. Like many things buried deeply in our ninety percent, we know all of this, but in our actual living, we strive to be transformed, then wonder what we did wrong when nothing seems to change.

Given this vicious cycle many of us find ourselves in, it is no wonder we are often frustrated and disillusioned with our Christian walk. By God's literal grace, however, learning to become aware of what's going on under the waterline of your habitual thoughts, behaviors, and actions can help you start to *think* differently. By the power of the Holy Spirit, the Lord will help you renew your mind as Paul encourages us to do in Romans 12:2, and in doing so, it will begin to move what you know about God and the Bible from your head more deeply into your bones.

Because learning to hear the gigantic part of our head that's under water, if you will, takes time, this response journal is designed to help you learn to reflect on what you notice, not repair it. The Oxford Dictionary defines "reflecting" as "to think deeply or carefully about, not to solve or fix."[6] Learning to pay attention to our ninety percent and asking the Lord about what we notice there is about developing *awareness*, not discovering *answers*. Becoming routinely aware of the subtle thoughts we have under the waterline of our own awareness in the monotonous parts of our everyday lives can help expose doubts we have about our faith. The ninety percent of our brain function that we are mostly unaware of is buried deeply. Since we did not arrive quickly at the disappointing place where many of us find our marriages, faiths, and views of ourselves, we will not quickly deconstruct the abstract beliefs that led us there. Therefore, we must continually ask the Lord to help us practice patience in this process. Pray also for help as you think deeply and carefully to resist the urge to solve anything you expose in the coming weeks.

---

[6] (Press, nd)

The Power of a Human

For the past two years, I've been using an app to learn to play the piano. When the notes and lessons were basic, the app worked fine. However, it was useless in assessing my timing or if my hands were in the correct position. Two weeks ago, I started taking lessons from a human, and to say that the difference is dramatic would be an understatement. Apart from the technical feedback Kendra gives me while I play, the most dramatic way human-to-human lessons are superior to computer-to-human ones is the immediate feedback my human gives me. As soon as I finish a melodic masterpiece like "Row, Row, Row Your Boat," Kendra tells me whether I played the accent notes correctly or not. She can instruct and coach me in the middle of a song without missing a beat, literally. However, the best part of Kendra's feedback is the encouragement she gives me. I know Kendra wants me to succeed and is honest about her assessments of my skills, so when she tells me I have a good sense of rhythm or that I'm playing my slurs correctly, it makes me not only want to keep playing and practicing, it makes me want to get better.

Learning the tenets and practices in this response journal is no different. Just as you can use an app to learn the basics of piano, you can read a book to learn how to expose doubt and believe deeper, but there's no substitute for human feedback and encouragement. To compensate for that, repetition will be prominent. In order to make paying attention to your ninety percent more habitual and encourage you as you learn and reflect, many phrases and pithy sayings in this book are intentionally repeated. I hope these recurring ideas will remind you that you are known and loved by the King of Kings, because according to Jesus, you are. He says that you are chosen (1 Thessalonians 1:4), equipped (Ephesians 2:10), and made complete in Him (Colossians 2:10). It is my prayer that reading these tenets again and again will help you know and believe more deeply these labels that He gave His Son to give to you.

Every chapter also ends with real-life examples illustrating the tenets and ideas you are responding to, praying about, and searching Scripture to deny or affirm. The most helpful humans who walk beside and ahead of us are usually calm and unflappable. They are not shocked by the things we discover in our ninety percent that feel repulsive and embarrassing to us. One of the biggest schemes of the enemy is making us think we are alone in our doubts and failures. When we keep those lies in the dark, they often morph and become more difficult to bring into the light of God's truth. It is my prayer that the reminders and repetitions in this book, along with the examples at the end of each chapter, will encourage you to keep listening for and moving toward God's love for you and remind you that the dark things in your ninety percent are not unusual.

Of course, if you are able to grab a godly sister, ideally one who is a few steps ahead of you in her faith walk, I encourage you to go through this journal with her. However, find a friend who does not default to flattering, fixing, or making you feel better, but rather points you to God's love and challenges you to do the same. Unlike learning to play the piano, the "goal" of exposing doubt and believing deeper is not to get better. A deeper knowing of ourselves and the Lord that helps us trust God in our actual living will ultimately and *organically* cause us to live in greater obedience, but that is not the goal. If it were the goal, Jesus would not have had to die for us in the first place. Later, we will talk more about how to walk alongside one another in exposing doubt and believing deeper by asking good questions like Jesus did. But for now, remember that giving people answers or advice or helping them avoid difficulty and pain does not usually help anyone experience transformation. It is only when we learn how to repeatedly submit and surrender to the good news of the cross of Christ in our actual lives that we will begin to believe deeper.

Faith Defined

Yesterday, I spoke to Jackie, a woman from my discipleship group who has been learning to pay attention to her unintentional thoughts, habits, and behaviors for the better part of a year, particularly as they related to her propensity to respond to her family in anger. As the two of us talked, she told me she had been feeling better about a recent conversation where she responded to her daughter with what she called "rage." Jackie had been paying attention to her ninety percent and asking the Lord about her response toward her daughter and felt like the Lord was "meeting her there." However, as she spoke about the conversation with her daughter and the aftermath of it, she got emotional. When I asked her why she was tearful in talking about the conversation, she paused thoughtfully, then said through her tears, "I feel like every time I shout at my family, it proves I'm not genuine and that I'm inconsistent in my faith."

When I asked Jackie what she meant by "faith," she said, "An abiding belief that Jesus is who He says He is. That He sacrificed for me and has forgiven me, and that He is the Son of God." I then asked her how she could be "inconsistent in her faith" if her faith did not have anything to do with what she did. "I guess my faith isn't about me. It's about Jesus," she said, "but I guess I just struggle to feel forgiven when I keep being inconsistent with my responses." Jackie knew the gospel of grace, and she could quickly and easily recite it perfectly, but she struggled to receive Christ's ongoing forgiveness for her actual past and present failures and conversations.

Pastor and theologian Alister McGrath said that in addition to faith uniting believers in a personal covenant with God, and it being an obedient response to the Word of God, "...faith has a personal reference. Simply to give cognitive assent to the historical facts surrounding the gospel cannot put a person into right relationship with God. Faith must be understood as having relevance for us personally"[7] (384-385). Many of us are like Jackie. We can easily and succinctly share our definition of faith in Jesus Christ, but that grace does not deeply intersect with our real-life relationships and ongoing mistakes. For many of us, faith is cognitively reasonable, but it isn't personally relevant.

Martin Luther said, "The article of justification must be sounded in our ears *incessantly* because the frailty of our flesh will not permit us to take hold of it perfectly and to believe it with all our heart"[8] (italics added, 12). How does faith become personally relevant? How do we incessantly sound the cross of Christ in our ears so we believe it with all of our heart? We can start by paying attention to the "frailty of our flesh." We can examine the "unintentional thoughts, actions, and behaviors" that expose where the gospel is *irrelevant* in our actual lives. That is what the focus of the first half of *Believe Deeper* is all about, helping you expose doubts and disconnects between what you believe deeply and what you are only giving "cognitive assent."

After we learn to practice paying attention to what's going on in our ninety percent, the second part of this response journal is intended to help you transform your faith by unearthing the "why" behind the doubts and disconnects you noticed in Part One. Part Two, however, is also about learning how to incessantly lean into God's love and labels, like being chosen, loved, and equipped. Labels that give us our new identity because of Christ's sacrificial death on the cross. I pray that *Believe Deeper* will help you learn, perhaps in a more unconventional way than you've learned before, to incessantly sound the article of justification in your ear, and in doing so, believe and experience Christ's grace and the freedom it affords you deeply in both your heart and your actual life.

---

[7] (McGrath, 1994)
[8] (Luther, 2011)

PART ONE

Expose Doubt: How and Why?

*"Christ never failed to distinguish between doubt and unbelief. Doubt
is can't believe. Unbelief is won't believe. Doubt is honesty. Unbelief is
obstinacy. Doubt is looking for light. Unbelief is content with darkness."*
Henry Drummond

Week One

BROKEN

"The growth of trees and plants takes place so slowly that it is not easily seen. Daily we notice little change. But, in course of time, we see that a great change has taken place. So it is with grace."
John Owen

"You have a fractured tibial plateau. You cannot put any weight on your leg for the next six weeks. See you December 22nd."

The doctor was so matter-of-fact about my impending incapacitation. He acted like it was not a big deal that I would be confined to my bed and a recliner for a month and a half. It was an inevitable lesson, I suppose. The amount of gray hair and brake pads I burned through over the years should have been indicators and motivators for me to slow down, but it took a biking accident. A biking accident where I didn't only break my tibia, I also fractured my wrist. A broken wrist meant no crutches or conventional walker for this girl. In order to leave my bed, I had to use a walker with a platform for my broken wrist. Although this would have been difficult for anyone, for type A, efficiency-driven me, it was incomprehensible. Literally. It would take me months to embrace something I had strategically and intentionally avoided for fifty-one years: moving slowly.

Functioning with a maimed body and at a snail's pace, not only for six weeks after my accident but for the six months it took me to (almost) completely rehab, forced me to slow down in every area of life. I could not do what I constantly, and with great frustration, implored my children to do when they were young: "Hurry up!" I could not walk faster when I was running behind, nor could I traverse any terrain other than flat. I had to clean my house, wrap Christmas presents (my accident was on November 7th), and do everything else *slowly*. I had to depend on others to help me with even the simplest of tasks. It was humbling and frustrating, but it was also wholly and entirely necessary. Although I hated every moment of it, being broken taught me lessons of gratitude and compassion for the hurting around me and, most importantly, the beauty of slowing down in a way I would not have otherwise learned.

The Not-so-Amazing Race

Our desire is to race. Even if you are not quite as hyper as I am, most Westerners are wired similarly, particularly when it comes to things like dieting, learning an instrument, or transforming faith. We want to lose, learn, and leap quickly. We want to take a few notes and rapidly move on to avoid pain and hardship. In our heads, where abstractions abound, we know that life is a marathon, not a sprint. We acknowledge that we have learned the most in life through hard times, and we understand that we cannot rush through the places God wants to take us, but when it comes to our actual lives, we are disappointed and stressed when we don't improve quickly.

The process of exposing doubt and transforming one's faith, if done correctly, is no different. Learning how to practice paying attention to your ninety percent can only be done slowly, as will asking the Lord about what you notice there and receiving His grace with what you find. In order to get where we want to be with what we believe about the Lord, it will benefit us to ask Him to help us be still. The best way to expose doubt and transform faith is to do so slowly, intentionally, and repeatedly.

Fortunately, you more than likely do not have a broken leg. You probably aren't physically incapacitated, and although you want to grow in your faith, you may not deeply desire or have the time to reflect in this response journal for hours on end. I, the great hoarder and coveter of time, fully understand and appreciate that dilemma. How do we move to a place of deep desire and change when we are not forced? How do we read the Bible and commune with God slowly when work, the kids, and our messy kitchens distract, detain, and drown out our best intentions? How do we slow down without falling hard?

Although you may not be visibly broken, if you are anything like me, your relationships and actual life on any given day can feel crippling. The decisions I have to make and conversations I need to have can sometimes feel exhausting and paralyzing. Often, just trying to read my Bible every day or parent without threatening to sell one of my children can seem like overwhelming and impossible tasks. Often, ordinary living makes me feel emotionally, relationally, and spiritually broken, and like the prodigal son, I become hungry and desperate enough to return to my Father. Often, God in His love allows us to feel so depleted that in our brokenness, we are forced to slow down.

It is my deep desire that you will go through this response journal in a way that will not perhaps feel natural to you. I pray you will traverse through the next several weeks slowly. I pray you will be able to reflect, "think deeply or carefully about, not to solve or fix," before you respond to the struggles and brokenness in your actual life. It is my hope that you will begin to receive deep healing in the emotional and spiritual places you may be hurting and experience peace as you attend to a deeper knowing of yourself and God, rather than trying to obtain quick answers. My prayer is that you will ask the Lord to help you slow down and reflect upon whatever He has for you, however that looks, whenever you can sit with Him. And as you do, the grace and love that infiltrates your heart in that stillness will incentivize you with the beauty that can often only be found when we slow down, and that it will keep you coming back for more.

Your Turn

Psalms 139:1-4 says, "You have searched me, Lord, and you know me. You know when I sit and when I rise; you perceive my thoughts from afar. You discern my going out and my lying down; you are familiar with all my ways. Before a word is on my tongue, you, Lord, know it completely." One commentator explained that what David is saying in this passage is "God, you know me perfectly, far beyond my knowledge of myself..."[9] (925). David recognized that our thoughts, actions, and ways are deep and complex. This is part of the reason why the Bible encourages us to take captive every thought and make it obedient to Christ (2 Corinthians 10:5b) and think about whatever is true, noble, right, pure, lovely, admirable, excellent, and praiseworthy (Philippians 4:8). How do we allow the Lord to search us? How do we renew our mind and keep it "stayed on" the Lord (Isaiah 26:3)? How do we think deeply and carefully about God's Word and slow down enough not to solve or fix anything, but just listen and pay attention? We practice.

Every day this week, practice reading and remaining in Psalms 139:1-4. If you do not already do so, pray before you read the Bible and ask the Spirit to help your mind be still and see whatever He has for you in His Word. As you read, write down any questions and thoughts that come to mind. Read the passage over and over until a thought, situation in your life, or a past conversation comes to mind.

---

[9] (*The NIV Study Bible*, 1984)

If nothing seems to stand out, do not give up praying and reading—
the Lord has something for you! Write down how you feel about the
Lord searching and knowing every thought you've ever had. Are you
proud or maybe embarrassed about Him knowing your every movement and what you talk about under your breath and aloud? Write
down any ideas or doubts you have or emotions you feel.

As you pay attention to your thoughts and life as you read Psalms
139:1-4 this week, be kind to yourself. Remember that Jesus offered
living water to the woman at the well in John 4 before she understood
or believed in Him. He told a criminal hanging on a cross next to
Him that he would join Jesus in paradise simply because he believed
that Jesus was who He said He was (Luke 23:40-43). Jesus forgave
Peter for disowning Him three times. Romans 4:7-8 says, "Blessed
are those whose transgressions are forgiven, whose sins are covered.
Blessed is the one whose sin the Lord will never count against them."
Regardless of your actual life—real feelings and responses—remind
yourself that you are already blessed and forgiven. Thanks to Jesus,
our sins will never count against us. Rest in that as you write down
anything you feel or notice as you read Psalms 139:1-4 slowly.

FOR EXAMPLE

Look! A Squirrel!

I woke up early and looked at the alarm clock. My to-do list ran through my head as I tried to repress the part of my brain reminding me that it was Saturday so I should keep sleeping. I got up, made a pot of coffee, and started reading Acts 7:44-53. I have learned over the past few years that reading my Bible before I do anything else is a good practice for a myriad of reasons. And since I've been practicing slowing down, one of the ways I've been doing that more often is by only reading a small portion of Scripture every day.

Before I begin reading God's Word at a snail's pace, I try to first remember to pray, "Spirit, help me see." I ask God to show up and enlighten my mind and my heart in a supernatural way. For many years, I've read the Bible hoping abstractly that the Spirit would help me see. In actuality, however, I was reading to learn and glean information. I would search cross references and commentaries to ensure I was understanding the context. I would sometimes look at maps or my Bible dictionary for further facts and clarification. For the better part of twenty years, I would read what is often affectionally called "A love letter from the Lord" like it was an encyclopedia or repair manual.

It is a rare occasion that after praying for the Spirit to help me see that something stands out the first time I read the passage. Oftentimes I have to read the text over and over. Today, after reading Acts 7:44-53 three times, I felt a Spirit-inspired nudge reminding me to practice something else that's been helping me slow down. I stopped reading and thought about the things lurking in my ninety percent that were distracting me: my work deadline, the bike ride I wished I could take instead of working on a Saturday morning, and the outfit I was going to wear to a graduation I was attending later in the day. Then I read the text yet again. This time, however, I looked for anything the Lord wanted me to pay attention to in my actual life relative to these distractions.

After the fourth time through, Acts 7:51b caught my eye: "You always resist the Holy Spirit." Because I have been learning to read the Bible not only slowly, but also trying to remember that there is "no condemnation for those who are in Christ Jesus" (Romans 8:1)—I stopped myself. I remembered that Stephen was directing this comment to the Jewish priests who were persecuting him, not Jesus' followers. As I paused, the Spirit reminded me that as a believer in Christ, I get to hear Acts 7:51b as an invitation, not a criticism. The Lord was not scolding me, but lovingly reminding me through this passage to ask the Holy Spirit into my publishing deadline, desire to find time to exercise, and eagerness to look good for strangers at the graduation.

The squirrels in my head are cute and easily grab my attention. My self-diagnosed ADD is rampant and real, so slowing down and creating space for the Lord is not my default. However, practicing praying and reading my Bible over and over in one sitting incentivizes me to do it more. Reading His Word prayerfully and repeatedly is not only forcing me to slow down, but it is also teaching me that doing so helps me reap personal and powerful insights and transformation in my actual life.

Week Two

ABSTRACT VERSUS CORE

"Jesus asked the boy's father, 'How long has he been like this?'
'From childhood,' he answered. 'It has often thrown him into fire or water
to kill him. But if you can do anything, take pity on us and help us.'
'If you can?' said Jesus. 'Everything is possible for one who believes.'
Immediately the boy's father exclaimed, 'I do believe;
help me overcome my unbelief!'"
Mark 9:21-24

Before I simultaneously broke my two appendages last year, I had no idea how painful fractures are and that walking again can take months. I also didn't know that what we break is never quite the same again. I realized after my accident, however, that it would have been impossible for me to understand. When my children have broken bones, I've taken them to and walked alongside them at doctor appointments, surgeries, and physical therapy, but that did not prepare me for how difficult it was to have and recover from my own fractured tibia. Knowing about something is never the same as experiencing it. Abstractly and empathetically, I knew a broken bone hurt. Conceptually, to the best of my ability, I understood that physical therapy was painful and recoveries were slow and arduous. But now I know from experience. My knowledge is no longer abstract and conceptual, but realized and concrete.

Tim Keller wrote, "There are many things Christians know but they don't really know. They know these things in part, but they haven't grasped them with the heart and had the imagination so captured that it has changed them thoroughly from the inside out"[10] (164). In life and faith, we abstractly believe many beneficial and morally upstanding things for ourselves and others. However, unless our beliefs are deeply and firmly rooted in our hearts in a way that changes how we speak, act, and think in our actual lives, they are not core beliefs.

In Mark 9, there is a father who believed, in part, that Jesus could help him and his son. How unimaginably painful it must have been for this father to watch his demon-possessed son be drowned and burned, year after year. It must have been tortuous to hope for healing, only to be disappointed. Waiting for healing that was not only physical, but for the mental and emotional trauma they both had experienced for so long. However, the father believed that if anyone could help them, perhaps Jesus, whom he'd probably heard so much about, could. But part of him did not believe. He believed in part, but he also needed help overcoming unbelief in the struggles of his actual life.

But imagine if the father had decided not to bring his son to Jesus because he was too embarrassed that he did not have a greater faith. The tragedy would have been missed freedom, safety, and abundant living for the father and his son. Although it usually feels embarrassing and shameful when we learn to listen to doubts and questions we have under the waterline of our own awareness, we must remember and trust Jesus' heart for us in our unbelief. Jesus met the father's

---

[10] (Keller, 2016)

partial belief as He meets yours and mine, with a willingness to help everyone trust and realize what His love and grace are meant to afford His followers in their actual lives, not just abstractly. Getting to the root of our unbelief and peeling back the layers that mask the source of our pain and dissatisfaction in life begin by honestly identifying what we only believe in part, no matter how difficult or embarrassing it may feel. Jesus will meet us as He did this young boy and his father, a boy once possessed by that which overtook and overwhelmed him, but who was lifted gently to his feet by Jesus, all because his father dared to believe deeper.

That's a Bully

Last week, you wrote down observations and questions you had as you read Psalms 139:1-4. Look back at what you wrote. How did you feel about the Lord searching and knowing every thought you've ever had? Were you proud or embarrassed thinking about Him knowing your every movement and what you talk about under your breath and aloud? What about conversations and situations in your actual life that you were distracted by or that related to the passage? Were you kind to yourself in those observations?

We know abstractly that there is no condemnation for those of us who are in Christ Jesus and that godly sorrow leaves no regret (2 Corinthians 7:10), but you might have felt last week a sense of embarrassment for things you thought, doubts you had, or that movie you watched on Friday night. We will talk more about the difference between condemnation and conviction in the next chapter, but for now, the easy way to distinguish between the two is that condemnation sounds like a bully and focuses on you, whereas God's loving conviction is compassionate and focuses on Christ's finished work at Calvary. Condemnation makes us want to run or hide, but conviction feels like a friend loving us enough to protect and care for us.

Last week's reflections may reveal that some of your beliefs about the finished work of the cross are not yet core beliefs, and that is not only okay, it's a good thing. The reality is most of us believe the message of the gospel in part; however, if you noticed anything that sounded like a bully in your unintentional thoughts as you read Psalms 139:1-4 last week, God is helping you step toward more freedom and a deeper belief. That may not feel good, but paying attention to where there is a disconnect between your abstract and core beliefs is a gift. Without realizing these disconnects that we all have, we might miss what the Lord has for us. We may be missing an opportunity to trust the Lord and see and feel the depth of His love more. Identifying doubts and partial and abstract beliefs is imperative to exposing the why behind many of our unintentional thoughts, habits, and actions and is an opportunity to be gently lifted to our feet by the One who came to give us life more abundant.

Your Turn

This week, while you are singing a worship song, reading your Bible, or listening to a sermon or podcast, ask yourself, "D.I.B.T.?" (Do I Believe That, a little initialism I came up with during a lengthy crisis of faith I had while in seminary). Do you believe the lyrics you are passionately singing on Sunday that God's *never* going to let you down? When you're sitting by a loved one in the ICU, do you believe deeply that God works out everything for the good of those who love Him and are called according to His purpose (Romans 8:28)? If you aren't sure if you fully believe that God is loving when you see someone suffering or that He is good when there's a pandemic, remember that Jesus doesn't respond to those doubts with guilt or shame. He wants to meet us where we authentically are and move our abstract beliefs to core ones in our actual lives.

As you pay attention to D.I.B.T this week, write down one thing you struggle to believe deeply about Christ or the Bible. Don't try to justify yourself or avoid the impending lightning strike you fear is headed your way. Tim Keller said, "A faith without some doubts is like a human body with no antibodies in it. People who blithely go through life too busy or indifferent to ask the hard questions about why they believe as they do will find themselves defenseless against either the experience of tragedy or the probing questions of a smart skeptic. A person's faith can collapse almost overnight if she failed over the years to listen patiently to her own doubts, which should only be discarded after long reflection."[11]

Remember that because of Christ's death on the cross, God does not hold your doubt and sin against you (Psalms 103:12). Write down everything you noticed this week that you struggled with when asking D.I.B.T. If you realize it's hard for you to trust the Lord with your husband's seemingly absent faith, your child's mental health issues, or even that dinner party you're hosting, be kind to yourself as you pay attention and reflect. Everyone has areas of doubt and partial beliefs, so pray and ask God to help you with any embarrassment or shame you may be noticing.

_____

_____

_____

_____

_____

_____

_____

_____

[11] (Keller, 2022)

FOR EXAMPLE

A Bad Mom

Cynthia's college-aged daughter had made several life choices recently that were, as Cynthia described them, "not in line with their family's Biblical beliefs." Cynthia and her husband had a good relationship with their daughter, and she was thriving in college and work, but they were struggling with some of their daughter's decisions as of late. She told me that it was difficult because their daughter had been raised in the church and knew how hard her decisions were on her parents. Cynthia confessed she did not want to deal with the situation. I asked her an obvious question to try and help her expose any abstract beliefs she had about the Lord or any lies she was believing about herself and her parenting. I asked her why she wished she did not have to deal with the situation and talk to her daughter about her choices.

Cynthia thought for a moment, then started tearing up. She said it was incredibly difficult and painful to watch her daughter make these choices. When I asked another seemingly obvious question, why her daughter's choices were painful to her, she looked off into the distance. Cynthia wiped her tears away and looked back at me with embarrassment. "I know in my mind this isn't true, but I suppose in some ways her choices are painful because they reflect poorly on me." Cynthia went on to say that she wondered where she went wrong in her mothering. She had thought over and over about what she could have done differently when her daughter was younger. She continued, "I know I cannot make my daughter's choices for her or be responsible for them, but I feel like a failure as a mother."

Although Cynthia believed that she was not responsible for her adult child's choices, it was only an abstract belief. She believed, in part, that every good work was from above and that God was in control. However, the reality of the sadness and regret she was experiencing regarding what she could have done differently in parenting revealed that these were abstract beliefs about the Lord. They were also core lies and sources of condemnation about her parenting.

Like Cynthia, we know that many things in our mind are not true about what we believe, but we do not know how to move those beliefs deeper. Identifying partial beliefs does not transform them into core ones simply because we begin to pay attention to them. But learning to recognize disconnects between what we know in our mind and the lack of peace and freedom we are experiencing in our actual lives is the first step in moving toward change.

Week Three

MAKING NEW TRACKS

"Do not conform to the pattern of this world, but be transformed by the renewing of your mind. Then you will be able to test and approve what God's will is—his good, pleasing and perfect will."
Romans 12:2

For many years, I have tried doing many things to implement Romans 12:2 and "renew my mind." I participated in Bible studies, memorized Scripture, and hung reminders around my house prompting me to start doing some things and stop doing others. I took copious notes at church and read many Christian books too. However, despite everything I tried to do to renew myself and my mind, I was not sure either was changing, and I certainly did not seem to be looking or feeling more like Jesus in my actual life.

There are many things in Scripture that remind us what to do and stop doing. Most of us appreciate the black-and-white nature of these kinds of verses, especially those of us who are rule followers. We believe, under the waterline of our awareness, that concrete dos and don'ts inform and assess how we are doing. They serve as subconscious litmus tests that provide an indicator of how well we are doing what the Bible tells us to do or not to do. However, since I cannot execute the things of the Bible perfectly no matter how hard I try, attempting to keep a scorecard of goodness does not tell me if what I am doing is good *enough*. Therefore, although I knew Romans 8:29 said I was being conformed to the likeness of Christ, I continuously beat myself up whenever I failed to perform or speak perfectly. Any improvements towards being less hostile toward my family while getting ready to leave for church, spending less time on social media, or reading my Bible every day seemed insufficient. I loved mandates in the Bible like James 3 reminding me to tame my tongue, but I didn't like wondering if two steps forward and seven back constituted tame *enough*. Unfortunately, that led to another problem with trying to assess if my behavior was good enough.

After over twenty years of trying to do the "dos" more and the "do nots" less, my inability to be successful at either, no matter how hard I tried, led to frustration and disillusionment. I wanted to stop losing my temper with my family, so I memorized Ephesians 4:26-27: "'In your anger do not sin': Do not let the sun go down while you are still angry, and do not give the devil a foothold." However, when I was running late or when my husband did not do that thing I asked him to do *exactly* as I'd asked him, I would blow my top. I remember reading and lamenting over 1 Peter 3:3-4: "[Wives], your beauty should not come from outward adornment, such as elaborate hairstyles and the wearing of gold jewelry or fine clothes. Rather, it should be that of your inner self, the unfading beauty of a gentle and quiet spirit, which is of great worth in God's sight." I wondered how someone like me, who wasn't born with a gentle *or* quiet spirit (and who loves accessories), could possibly ever live this out. Despite asking the Lord for help, I was almost constantly frustrated and disappointed with myself.

How do we renew our minds? How are we transformed deeply? Certainly, memorizing Scripture, participating in Bible studies, and asking the Lord for help are wonderful and effective means. Hiding God's Word in our heart matters, and nothing can replace ensuring that we know and are armed with God's truth at all times. However, Hebrews 4:2 says, "For unto us was the gospel preached, as well as unto them: but the word preached did not profit them, *not being mixed with faith* in them that heard it" (KJV, italics added). Many of us read the Bible. Some of us even commit it to memory. We know and have had the Bible preached to us, but until we slow down and ask God to help us see where Scripture is penetrating and challenging our actual lives, it may not be profiting us. Trusting the Lord more deeply happens as we repeatedly submit and surrender to Christ's love and forgiveness for us in the brokenness of our actual relationships and stresses. That evolving trust transforms our faith in a way that trying harder never can.

What does it look like to renew our minds? How do we not only hide God's Word in our heart, but move what we believe about His Word from a place of conceptual abstractions to core beliefs that impacts our heart? If trying harder and memorizing more Scripture do not seem to lead to the transformation we are hoping for, what does it look like to surrender to what Jesus has given us on the cross? Do we just curl up in the fetal position and wait? Do we revert to osmosis and try sleeping on our Bibles? As someone I'm discipling just asked me, "Why try harder to do anything if renewing our mind and looking more like Jesus isn't about what we do, but what Jesus already did on the cross? What does that even look like?" It looks like sledding.

Making New Tracks

Several years ago, we hosted an international high school student from China. Jun was from the southern part of the country where it rarely snowed, so when we had our first good old-fashioned Wisconsin snowstorm of the year, he wanted to go sledding. After he wiped out on the big hill, Jun wanted to try something a little tamer. When we got to the bunny hill, there were several tracks made by veteran sledders earlier in the day, but because Jun had never gone sledding before, he put his sled down in the deep, untouched snow. When he laid down on the sled, the walls of snow that formed around the perimeter of our two-hundred-pound JV wrestler collapsed around him. Determined to have fun, though, Jun used his arms in a butterfly motion to push himself slowly and arduously down the hill. The deep snow spilled into the collar of his jacket. His glasses started to fog up. His wrists were bright red where his mittens stopped and sleeves began. No matter how hard he thrust his arms, the snow seemed to render the laws of gravity and inertia useless, but Jun was undeterred. When he finally got to the bottom of the hill, Jun ran smiling back to the top of the path he'd just trenched and got back on his sled. This time, he went down a little faster and with less snow going down the front of his jacket. Every time Jun went down, the track got deeper and more fun.

Science confirms what Scripture tells us in Romans 12:2 and what Jun illustrated on the sledding hill: we can make new tracks. When we repeatedly think or behave in new ways, our brains literally "change in response to behavior" as we form neural pathways that alter the chemical, structural, and functional levels of the brain.[12] Although longstanding repetitive thoughts and actions have formed deep tracks in our brain, we do not have to return to those existing pathways. However, just like with sledding, creating new tracks in the form of new ways of thinking about God and who He says we are is not easy. It is faster and there is less resistance going down existing tracks, but there is also less transformation when we continue to descend down paths laden with lies and abstract beliefs.

How do we renew our minds? One way is by learning to notice what's going on in our ninety percent. Prayerfully becoming more aware of our unintentional thoughts, behaviors, and actions helps

---

[12] (Call, 2019)

us identify the deep, familiar tracks we return to that are not in line with the truth of who God is and says we are. In practicing paying attention to our ninety percent, we will be able to expose tracks we detest but can't seem to stop going down. We can begin to renew our minds by replacing lies we believe about ourselves and partial truths we believe about the Lord with new tracks of who God says we are. The more we practice returning to the Biblical truth of who God says we are instead of the condemnation and lies we say about ourselves, the deeper the tracks of truth will get. But we have to start by paying attention to and identifying current tracks to which we habitually return, tracks that have become deeply embedded without any conscious awareness that we were making them in the first place.

Your Turn

Making new tracks on a sledding hill and in our brains takes time, patience, and repetition. The only way to stop returning to the longstanding lies we believe about ourselves is to continue making *new* tracks in line with the truth of Scripture and going down them over and over again. Practice never makes perfect when it comes to creating neural pathways, but practice does lead to new ways of thinking and acting more frequently. Practice not only deepens new tracks in line with Scripture, but it also ensures we go down the old tracks less, which are inconsistent with how God sees and defines us.

One of the ways I've learned to create new tracks is to read the Bible better. Before I learned to pay attention to the difference between abstract and core beliefs in my heart and mind, I used to read the Bible to find out how to be a better mom, wife, and human. I scoured the pages of Scripture, trying to discern how I could stop having road rage or caring so much about the condition of my house. My Bible was filled with highlighted verses about getting rid of all bitterness, rage, and malice, and other dos and don'ts I *should* work on. Before I began to know God's love made manifest at the cross more deeply, I read the Bible like it was a behavior modification manual. However, apart from first deeply receiving and knowing the love and acceptance of Christ on the cross, trying harder seemed to result in disappointment over and over again, and it led to me hearing Scripture as condemnation instead of as a loving invitation.

Reading the Bible better is about reading the Bible to find out more about God's heart and character. It is to prayerfully see God's Word through the lens of His love for mankind, rather than reading it to find out how to fix ourselves. Reading the Bible better is simply reading it to know God and His love better. It is reading the creation narrative in Genesis 1 and thinking about His love and generosity for us in its beauty and intentional design. It is reading about Israel's liberation from slavery in Exodus 12 and remembering that freedom for Israel and for us through Jesus, our Passover lamb, is possible only because of the depth of God's love and care for us. Reading the Bible better is combing slowly through Jesus' prayer for us in John 17:20-26 and getting a picture of His heart for everyone who would believe in His name.

This week, read the Bible as it was intended—a love letter of redemption from a Father to His children. A love that, as it fills us up to overflowing and replaces the lies we believe with the truth of how God sees us, organically transforms us as we submit and surrender to His love for us, demonstrated by His sacrificial death (1 John 4:9-10). If you're not sure where to begin, you can start by reading Genesis 1, Exodus 12, or John 17. Write down any observations, questions, or tangents your brain took you down this week as you read your Bible better.

_____

_____

_____

FOR EXAMPLE

No Name Calling

It was a brilliant mothering moment. I overheard one of my kids calling themselves stupid. I told them that it made me sad to hear them calling themselves names and describing themselves in a way that Jesus never would. However, a few weeks later, I had misplaced my key fob, again. A few years ago, I had lost my key, and it cost hundreds of dollars to replace it. As I frantically headed to my closet to scour through my pants and jacket pockets, I heard a subtle condemning voice going on under the waterline of my awareness.

"You're so stupid."

"Why are you so unorganized?"

"How do you function as an adult when you lose everything?"

"I'm surprised Chris (my husband) trusts you with anything."

Then almost immediately, I heard another voice. It was me telling my kids not to call or say anything about themselves Jesus would never say about them. I had started going down the old, deep track of condemning and demonizing how and who God made me. I started listening to names and descriptions that Christ died to ensure *no one* could call me. Not even me. I was going down old tracks.

Learning to listen and notice when my unintentional, habitual thoughts, behaviors, and actions are not in line with who God is and says I am is helping me make new tracks. Paying attention to the thinking that goes on in my ninety percent is making me more aware of when I descend down old tracks that are incongruent with the Word of God. When I couldn't find my keys, and I heard that bully's voice in my ninety percent, I was able to take that thought captive and "make it obedient to Christ" (2 Corinthians 10:5b) by remembering that Jesus would never call me dumb or forgetful. I was able to move Christ's grace from an abstract to a core belief in my actual life.

I still lose things. I still speak before thinking at times and lose my temper, but my responses to those mistakes are finally beginning to look different more often. When we aren't aware of the lies we've habitually believed and thought about ourselves, it is difficult to stop making those tracks deeper. Becoming aware of thought patterns and lies I've defaulted to under the waterline of awareness is helping me not return to them as often. Remembering to descend and slowly create new tracks is beginning to give me freedom, peace, and joy that I've never been able to experience by trying harder.

Why? Because making new tracks is merely submitting and surrendering to who God says I am. It is recognizing when I am giving myself labels other than ones the Bible says about me regardless of my sin and failures. If I never identify the lies and abstract beliefs I'm consistently returning to, how can I pray about and replace those tracks with ones congruent with who Christ says I am because of His finished work on the cross?

Oswald Chambers said, "After we have been perfectly related to God in sanctification, our faith has to be worked out in actualities." One way we can renew our mind is to pay attention to our ninety percent as we go about our everyday lives. Recognizing when we are responding in a way that is contradictory to the gospel provides us an opportunity to know the height, width, length, and depth of Christ's love for us more and more. As we deepen those tracks of truth about who Christ says we are, His acceptance and forgiveness begin to overflow into the actualities of our lives.

Week Four

GOD'S DISPOSITION

"Don't you believe that I am in the Father, and that the Father is in me? The words I say to you I do not speak on my own authority. Rather, it is the Father, living in me, who is doing his work. Believe me when I say that I am in the Father and the Father is in me..."
John 14:10-11a

Charles Templeton not only preached with Billy Graham, but some predicted he would someday overshadow Graham as an evangelist. However, after battling doubt for many years, Templeton could not reconcile that God was good when there was such terrible suffering in the world. When author Lee Strobel interviewed Templeton years after he had become an agnostic, Templeton explained his dramatic theological reversal. "I began to think further about the world being the creation of God. I started considering the plagues that sweep across parts of the planet and indiscriminately kill—more often than not, painfully—all kinds of people, the ordinary, the decent, and the rotten. And it just became crystal clear to me that it is not possible for an intelligent person to believe that there is a deity who loves"[13] (14). When Strobel later asked Charles Templeton about Jesus, however, Templeton's demeanor and posture changed dramatically. He said that Jesus was the greatest human who ever lived and that He was the most important thing in his life. So much so that later, with tears in his eyes, Templeton "uttered words I [Strobel] never expected to hear from him. 'I . . . miss . . . him!'"[14] (18).

When I read about Charles Templeton years ago in an apologetics class in seminary, I thought it was incredibly strange that Templeton did not believe in a loving, caring, omniscient God but loved and missed Jesus Christ. Didn't Templeton know that God, Jesus, and the Holy Spirit comprised the same Triune God? Didn't he know that John 14 affirmed that Jesus is in the Father and the Father is in Him? Although my disconnect between God the Father and God the Son was not as extreme or egregious as Templeton's, after learning to pay more attention to what was going on in my ninety percent, I realized my view of God the Father was also very different than my view of His Son and that many of my own beliefs about the Triune God were only abstractions as well.

Disappointed

Perhaps it was being the daughter of a U.S. serviceman. Maybe it was being raised by a mother who was from Japan, where, culturally, shame was a primary motivator and disciplinary technique. Regardless, I have always had a picture of God that was very punitive and retributive. Under the waterline of my own awareness, I had a view of the Father that, like Templeton's, did not look anything like my view of Jesus. I thought God was either already disappointed with me for something I'd said or done or that He would be disappointed with me as soon as I messed up. I lived with the almost constant,

---

[13] (Strobel, 2000)
[14] (Strobel, 2000)

subconscious pressure and knowledge that I was not living up to who God wanted me to be.

During discipleship, I began to realize the extent to which my view of God was tainted. Although the Lord had been slowly revealing my skewed perception of Him a few years prior to the discipleship class, it was my friend Patricia who really helped me start to understand the dichotomy of my view of God the Father and God the Son. There were many things that led to my awareness of my tainted view of the Father, but two things stood out in particular as I practiced paying attention to my ninety percent in this area.

The first happened when I was struggling with a homework assignment I was given in the discipleship group that Patricia facilitated. Patricia had been paying attention to what was going on in her ninety percent for a few years. She knew that many of the things she believed were only abstract beliefs. She had experienced a great degree of freedom in learning to pay attention to what she only believed in part, so it was fairly obvious to her when she began walking alongside me in discipleship that there was a disconnect between what I knew in my mind about Christ's forgiveness and how I lived. I said and believed, in part, that I was saved through faith by grace. Jesus' work on the cross was finished, and I knew abstractly that there was nothing I could do to make Him love or accept me more. However, Patricia heard how hard I was on myself. She noticed how difficult it was for me to receive a compliment. For several months during discipleship, she had heard me share how defensive I was toward my husband. Although I knew and thought I fully believed that I was not striving or trying to earn God's favor, Patricia quickly saw a disconnect between my abstract and core beliefs, between what I said and how I spoke and acted. So, she gave me homework. She asked me to spend time enjoying God. If God was already pleased with me and couldn't love me more because of what Christ had done on the cross, I should be able to abstain from "doing" for Him.

Sadly, however, I had no idea what Patricia was asking me to do. I had no clue what it meant to just *be* with God. The other women in my discipleship group offered suggestions. One said that she "just sat with the Lord" by simply imagining being on her Daddy's lap enjoying His presence. I did not understand why one would do such an unproductive exercise, nor how one would have the attention span to do so. Another woman said she enjoyed being with God while gardening. Besides the fact that I kill things with green leaves, I did not see how that activity could be related to "enjoying God." I realized during the next several months of trying to understand and implement "enjoying God" that my view of God was not in line with what Scripture said about Him. Although I *knew* I didn't have to "do" anything for the Lord, I lived with the constant pressure that unless I was doing something *for* God, doing it consistently and doing it well, He was disappointed with me.

The second thing that helped me realize that my view of the Father was not one of a caring, on-my-side God was a conversation I overheard during the discipleship group. Patricia was talking to another woman about learning to hear God more intimately and personally. The woman's homework was whenever she was feeling stressed in the context of a particular relationship she was struggling in, she should repeat a Bible verse that she felt would help her make a new track in line with how God saw her. Before she read or recited the verse to herself, she was supposed to say her name first. "Karen, you are not the sum of your past mistakes. I love you, and I have made you a new creation."

Then Patricia told Karen that when she repeated the Bible verse, she should not only use her name, but also try to imagine the Lord saying the passage to her, like Karen would say it to her own daughter. The thought of God imploring us to feel His love, using the same fervor and genuineness I would use to convince my children of this message, made me tear up. I'd never thought of picturing God talking to me like that. I again realized my view of the Father was not the same as my view of Jesus. Like Templeton, my view of God was that of a harsh, disappointed disciplinarian. He wasn't a sweet, hold-your-hand-and-give-you-a-hug kind of Dad. He was a strict and distant one. It was no wonder I could not imagine enjoying time with Him.

Reconciling the Old Testament

I think my view of the Father has been shaped, in part, by the Old Testament, where God seemed stern, wrath-filled, and frequently doled out punishment to His followers. I have struggled with the sternness of God as He dealt with Moses when he struck a rock (Numbers 20:10-13), when Uzzah took hold of the ark of God (2 Samuel 6:1-7), and with Jephthah's vow to the Lord (Judges 11:30-40). Under the waterline of awareness, without any conscious intention or realization, God the Father was always waiting for me to make a mistake or be disobedient. I had a picture of Him that was generally disappointed with me.

If we were having coffee right now, I would imagine you might have some questions for me. Questions about whether or not I learned how to enjoy God, and if I did, what that looked like. Perhaps you resonated with my view of the God of the Old Testament. Maybe you would want to know if and how I reconciled the dichotomy I felt between God and Jesus. The bad news is I would not be able to answer those questions easily or sufficiently. Additionally, if I could somehow share perfectly and clearly how I arrived at the place where my view of God mirrors that of Jesus, it would not help you make that a core belief. You will have to reconcile and understand for yourself the depth of the love God has for you.

The good news is that I began to trust and step toward God's deep kindness toward me slowly and increasingly. Learning to trust God's character is not something we can or need to do quickly. We know that abstractly, but in our core, we are disappointed when we do not have a new picture of God's heart for us after a week of praying about it. Although slow and subtle, the shift of your view of God in line with Scripture—learning to pay attention to your real beliefs about God's demeanor and heart toward you—will be time well spent. And remember, Jesus did not meet the father's partial belief in Mark 9 with shame or disgust. He met the man where he actually was and led him to deeper belief out of His love and care. He will meet you where you really are without shame or condemnation too.

Your Turn

God's disposition to us is something we will discuss again, because if our view of the Father is tainted, it will be a major barrier to believing deeper. If we do not continually trust that God knows and loves us deeply, we will continue to trust Him and His Word abstractly. If we do not see or feel God in a way that lines up with the truth of His goodness and love for mankind, it will be difficult for us to realize the kind of faith and transformation we genuinely desire but often fail to experience in our actual lives.

This week, spend time enjoying the Lord. If you're like I was and have no idea what that means or looks like, just spend time enjoying yourself. Go on a long, slow walk or sit in your backyard. If you feel thankful during that time, tell the Lord that, but otherwise, just be still. We always think we want time to relax and enjoy, but the reality is we make time for what is important to us and do not make time to simply be. This may be a very difficult assignment for many of you, but try to practice enjoying God for at least ten minutes.

Journal what you did to enjoy the Lord or be still. How did it feel? Was it easy or difficult? Why do you think that was? Write down if you felt anxious, pressured, or distracted in your stillness. Jot down any time you felt like you *should* be doing something more productive. What was God's attitude toward you as you simply enjoyed

Him? Was He smiling or stoic? You do not need to explain or defend your observations. Remember that you are experimenting with and learning how to enjoy the Lord. This may take months, like it did for me. Our goal is to come to the Father as we are, not once we are cleaned up. If enjoying the Lord doesn't go well or happen at all, just write down what you notice and pray for help. He wants you to enjoy time just being with Him even more than you do, and He can't love you any more or any less.

_____

_____

_____

_____

_____

_____

_____

_____

_____

_____

_____

_____

_____

_____

_____

_____

FOR EXAMPLE

The Wink

A few weeks ago, we started watching the television series *The Chosen*. I had heard many things about it, but for whatever reason had never watched it. The first episode was good, and although it seemed like many other theatrical renditions I had seen about the Bible and life of Jesus, there was something different about it. The acting was better than most, and the storyline played out in way I had never seen before. The ending also left me wondering what would happen next, so I watched it again the following night.

In the second episode, Jesus was sitting at a table with Mary, a blind woman, and three men. While they talked, someone made a joke. Jesus smiled at the man and winked at him. That wink made my eyes fill with tears. Although I had been growing exponentially in surveying my attitude and perception of the Lord during discipleship and beyond, God, in His love, used a simple wink to expand my imagination for more. That non-cheesy, non-creepy, non-condescending, but genuine and very *human* wink stirred my affections for Christ deeply.

The next day, however, under the waterline of my awareness, I questioned this portrayal of Jesus. Was it Biblical? Did Jesus wink, laugh, make jokes, and dance? Did He interact with children tenderly and with a sense of humor, as He did in *The Chosen*? Was this a stretch? Although the abstractions I had about Jesus' love and grace for me were ever widening, I never pictured him dancing at a wedding. As I prayed about that, Genesis 1:26a came to mind. "Then God said, "Let us make mankind in our image, in our likeness . . ." The Triune God made man in His likeness. Why is it a stretch, therefore, to think that Jesus would not have laughed with or hugged others just as we do?

Until we are able to begin moving abstract views and ideas about the grace of Christ down into our core, it will be difficult to believe deeper. To imagine a stoic and always serious Jesus being on our side looks and feels different than a Jesus who laughs, hugs, and winks at you. Although the Lord has increasingly been helping me have a view of Him that is more consistent with who the Bible says He is, I realized in a wink that there is still room in my heart and imagination for more.

Week Five

THAT SOUNDS LIKE CONDEMNATION

"A legally convinced person cries out, 'I have exasperated a power that is as the roaring of a lion . . . I have provoked one that is the Sovereign Lord of heaven and earth whose word can tear up the foundation of the world . . .' But an evangelically convinced person cries, 'I have incensed the goodness that is like the dropping of a dew. I have offended a God that had his hands stretched out to me as a friend.'"
Stephen Charnock

Linda loved serving in ministry and was grateful her husband had left his career in the corporate world years ago to become a pastor. However, it had been several years since they were able to afford spending money on something aesthetic in their house, so Linda was thrilled when they decided to remodel their bathroom. She did not feel like she had a particularly good eye for decorating, but she was pleased at how their remodeling project was coming along. Until the scratch.

Linda's husband James accidentally put a mark in the countertop when he was installing the sink. Linda tried hiding her disappointment, but to no avail. When James insinuated that Linda was materialistic, she got extremely upset. I asked her why James' comment upset her as she sheepishly shared the story with me and the discipleship group I was facilitating. She thought about it for a moment, then said it was upsetting because it was probably the worst thing James could have called her. When I asked her why being materialistic was so terrible, she answered, "Because a Christian shouldn't be materialistic, should they?" I then asked Linda about wealthy King Solomon. When the queen of Sheba visited Solomon, she found him to be as wealthy as he was wise and said, "Praise be to the Lord your God, who has delighted in you and placed you on the throne of Israel" (1 Kings 10:9a). Linda acknowledged that perhaps one could be wealthy and a Christ follower. She looked off into the distance thoughtfully and, with a fearful look in her eyes, asked, "But what if I *am* materialistic? Isn't it possible to be concerned with nice things more than I'm focusing on delighting in God?"

What's the Difference?

In 2 Corinthians 7, Paul differentiates between godly and worldly sorrow. He says that godly sorrow leads us to repentance and salvation and "leaves no regret" (v. 10). On the other hand, worldly sorrow brings death. The NIV Commentary Bible explains the dichotomy between these two kinds of sorrows: "The former [godly sorrow] manifests itself by repentance and the experience of divine grace; the latter [worldly sorrow] brings death because, instead of being God-centered sorrow over the wickedness of sin, *it is self-centered sorrow over painful consequences of sin*"[15] (italics added, 1771).

Godly sorrow brought about by loving conviction reminds us of Christ's forgiveness and the identity He has given us because of His death. Worldly sorrow brought about by condemnation keeps us focused on our sin and ourselves. When we look inward and focus

---

[15] (*The NIV Study Bible*, 1984)

on our shortcomings, under the waterline of awareness, there is a quiet, subtle part of us that believes those failures, or the perception of them, make us look bad, prove we'll never get "better," and devalue our worth. Rather than standing on the firm and unchanging identity the Bible says God has given us because of Christ's death on the cross, we condemn ourselves. Instead of regularly preaching Christ's forgiveness and grace, we chastise ourselves for what we should or should not have done. Godly sorrow points us to Christ's finished work on the cross because of and simultaneously *regardless* of what we do. Worldly sorrow points to our mistakes and makes avoiding and improving them our primary concern.

If Linda, in fact, does care more about wealth or bathroom countertops, the Lord will *convict* her. Conviction is God's *kindness* leading us toward repentance (Romans 2:4b), and it is God's love that precedes and motivates His forgiveness (Psalms 103:8-12). Conviction isn't shameful or accusatory. It should feel like loving correction, not something we should be defensive or ashamed of. When the Lord convicts us out of His mercy, it is meant for our good and His glory. Romans 8:31-33 says, "What, then, shall we say in response to these things? If God is for us, who can be against us? He who did not spare his own Son, but gave him up for us all—how will he not also, along with him, graciously give us all things? Who will bring any charge against those whom God has chosen? It is God who justifies. Who then is the one who condemns? No one. Christ Jesus who died—more than that, who was raised to life—is at the right hand of God and is also interceding for us."

Unfortunately, condemnation is almost exclusively how many of us hear and feel God's correction. Merriam-Webster defines the word "condemn" as "to declare to be reprehensible, wrong, or evil usually after weighing evidence and without reservation."[16] Condemnation makes us feel guilt and shame because it causes us to take our eyes off

---

[16] (Merriam-Webster, 2022)

of Jesus' finished work on the cross. Condemnation puts the focus on our failures that we deem as "evidence" of our unworthiness.

Paying attention to Linda's emotions helped her see that she was actually upset because she felt James was confirming the voice of condemnation judging and accusing her. Linda realized the reason she was offended and hurt when James said she was materialistic was that she was embarrassed. She was afraid he was right. She mis-believed that wanting a nice bathroom counter devoid of scratches made her superficial and a "bad Christian." She believed James had weighed the evidence against her and declared her to be reprehensi-ble and wrong. But in reality, according to Scripture, not even Linda herself can condemn those who believe in Jesus Christ.

But That's Impossible

Romans 3:23-24 says, "For all have sinned and fall short of the glory of God, and all are justified freely by his grace through the redemption that came by Christ Jesus." Justification means we are no longer guilty; therefore, it is impossible for those of us who call Jesus Lord of our lives to be declared reprehensible or evil. Read that again. We tend to gloss over things in Scripture that seem true and obvious; however, let the truth of God's Word seep into your core for a moment. God's settled and unchanging disposition to us has been established by Christ's work on the cross. There is nothing we can do to change that. Most of us know that abstractly, but if we pay attention to the voice in our ninety percent, it will help us identify if Christ's death and resurrection is a core belief. Under the water-line of awareness, when you experience lust, watch that racy movie, or blow up at your spouse, do you bully and shame yourself? Or does sorrow come from knowing that Jesus died for and has so much more for you because of the depth of His love?

What do you do when you mess up? How do you feel? Are you frustrated and disappointed with yourself? Under the waterline of awareness, are you ashamed, feel like a poser or a hypocrite? Do you try to memorize another verse about keeping your cool or putting a guard over the door of your mouth because the last five verses you learned don't seem to be working? Or when you fail and do that thing you hate *again*, do you repent, trusting God's forgiveness and giving thanks for Christ's finished work on the cross? Do you think and look more at you or at Jesus when you mess up? God's conviction makes us sorry that we acted outside the character and identity that Christ, our brother and friend, died to give us. However, it does not bully us into believing we have out-sinned the cross or failed one too many times, or warrant a new identity other than the one Christ has given us once and for all.

Your Turn

One way we can begin to distinguish between hearing accusation and condemnation or love and conviction is to hear your head when you're a hot mess. When you make a mistake, how do you talk to and about yourself in your ninety percent? How do you sense the Lord is looking at you? When you swear in front of your kids on the way to church, do you feel embarrassed, under the waterline of awareness, to sing worship songs once you get to your seat? What is God's heart for you when you judge the outfit of the new, annoyingly pretty woman at your office? When you think of your divorce, do you beat yourself up for your part in it? Do you sense God's love or disappointment toward you because of it? Write down anything you notice.

Resist the urge to fix or explain what you observe. Just pay attention to how you talk to yourself and write it down. We will spend a significant amount of time taking all of this to the Lord, but for now, just listen. Pay attention to the thoughts you have about yourself that go on under the waterline of awareness when you mess up. If it gets to be too much, ask the Lord for help. He is compassionate and abounding in love for you, even and especially when you're at your worst.

I gave this assignment to a junior in high school, and she returned after one week and said that the bully in her head that's condemning and accusatory is "constant." Most of you are probably older than sixteen. You have been calling yourself names and demonizing yourself much longer than my young mentee. It may take some time to realize just how relentless you are in assigning names and motives to yourself that are not in line with who God says you are because of Christ's death on the cross. Although this exercise may feel difficult, remember it is good news to identify anything going on under the waterline of awareness that is not in line with the truth of God's Word!

_____

_____

_____

_____

_____

_____

_____

_____

_____

_____

_____

_____

_____

_____

FOR EXAMPLE

Go Sit Down

In Luke 14:7-11, Jesus talks about taking a seat at a wedding at the lowest place rather than in a place of honor. He explained to the Pharisees why compassion dictated the rule of the Law, and He chastised them for their arrogance in desiring the seat of honor in the first place. When I read that passage recently, I thought of my friend Sheryl. Her husband had passed away, and she asked me to arrive at the funeral early. She wanted me to check in with one of her kids who'd been struggling and be there for her if she needed anything. I told her I would be there for whatever she needed. I arrived at the church early and stayed near the front by Sheryl and her family for the visitation and service.

However, about halfway through the service, I heard a narrative playing in my head that had been going on under the waterline of my own awareness. I felt self-conscious about being in the front of the church. Deep in the recesses of my ninety percent, there was a voice saying, "You shouldn't be up here. Sheryl has other friends closer than you that should be with her," and then I heard another subtle condemning thought that someone said to me once when I was a very young girl: "You are being a show-off."

Fortunately, because I had practiced paying attention to my ninety percent for several years, I recognized the voice of the accuser in my head. Jesus never speaks in a shame-filled and finger-pointing way when He gently and lovingly corrects me, so I began to pray about feeling embarrassed. I asked the Lord to help me focus on Sheryl and remember that my validation comes from Him (Psalms 17:2).

After the funeral, Sheryl thanked me. "Seeing you there made me feel better," she said. The problem with the voice of condemnation that lurks subtly, but constantly, under the waterline of mental awareness is that it is sneaky and pervasive. It assigns blame and demonizes our motives. It tries to highlight the things we fear most about ourselves and reminds us of things from days or decades ago that made us feel embarrassed and wounded. The voice of condemnation is always trying to create distraction and doubt about who Christ says we are by trying to shift our focus off of Christ's finished forgiveness and onto our failures, real or imagined. The voice of condemnation always seems louder than God's truth in my mind, but paying attention more often is starting to change that. It is helping me make new tracks. Tracks that are in line with the truth of who I am because of the cross.

Week Six

IDENTITY MATTERS

"No, grace is non-contributory, and faith is the opposite of self-regarding. The value of faith is not to be found in itself, but entirely and exclusively in its object, namely Jesus Christ and him crucified."[17] (117)
John R. W. Stott

Dutch Catholic priest Henri Nouwen says there are three "very human lies" we believe about our identity: I am what I have, I am what I do, and I am what other people say or think about me.[18] If I have an impressive job title or my kids are on the honor roll, I feel good about myself. Unfortunately, the converse is also true. If my house isn't as fancy as yours or my car is old, I may struggle with jealously or embarrassment under the waterline of awareness. Identity is a significant place to learn to pay attention to our ninety percent. Why? Because we generally struggle to admit or believe that we derive our identity from such seemingly petty, material things.

---

[17] (Stott, 1994)
[18] (Nouwen, 1992)

However, the more I've paid attention to my ninety percent, the more I've realized my identity isn't usually grounded in who God says I am, but in what I have, want, and do.

If you are willing and brave enough to pay attention to what's going on in your ninety percent, you may realize, like me, that you feel better or worse about yourself and your standing with the Lord and with people based on things other than the cross. I believed Jesus died for me on the cross at Calvary to forgive me of my sins yesterday, today, and tomorrow. I taught my children Hebrews 10:17-18, "…their sins and lawless acts I will remember no more. And where these have been forgiven, there is no longer any sacrifice for sin." However, as I began to hear my head when I was a hot mess and pay attention to my ninety percent, I began seeing some disconnects.

When I would yell at my kids or swear at the driver cutting me off in traffic, I would subconsciously and relentlessly beat myself up. I felt like a failure as a parent and human being, not just because I failed, but because I failed as a Christian. The only thing worse than failing when I should have known better was the inability to quit failing. I believed Christ died to give me my unsettled and unchanging identity, but the more I paid attention to my unintentional, habitual thoughts, behaviors, and actions in my actual life, the more I realized I only believed in part. I would try to change and live W.W.J.D., but seemed never to be able to do so longer than about one day.

A few years ago, however, I learned a visual that helped me make new tracks and renew my mind in the area of identity in my actual life.[19] There isn't anything magical about this shape; it is merely a concrete way to see the gospel and help us move abstract beliefs about the identity we are given because of the cross to core ones. Although it may seem obvious and straightforward, perhaps it is its simplicity that makes it so eye-opening when it comes to

---

[19] (Breen, 2010)

explaining how many of us bypass the cross of Christ without even realizing it. I encourage you to remember as you read these seemingly basic tenets of the Christian faith to do so slowly, prayerfully, and reflectively.

1) God the Father

The graphic starts with God the Father on top. God is positioned on the triangle as we would agree He exists in our lives, personhood, and faith: at the head. Everything stems from the Father, which is why we spent time in Chapter Four talking about our view of Him. If, under the waterline of awareness, our view of God the Father is that of a wrath-filled God waiting to smite and discipline us, that will impact everything else. Our identity in Christ may seem solid and secure, but if we do not feel we are deeply loved and accepted by God the Father, it will likely taint how we hear, believe, and live out the gospel message.

(1) God the Father

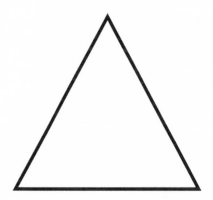

2) The Cross of Christ

From the Father, we move to knowing and accepting Jesus Christ's death and resurrection on the cross. We trust that by believing in Jesus Christ, we are forgiven of our sins (John 3:16). We know that to be saved means to confess with our mouth that Jesus is Lord and believe in our hearts that God raised Him from the dead (Romans 10:9). We hold fast to what it says in John 5:24, that by hearing God's Word and believing in Christ, we have crossed over from death to life. The grace and forgiveness of Christ on the cross is the gateway to freedom and righteousness. (For those of you good, churchgoing, Bible-reading folks out there who may be wondering why we need a shape to explain the obvious truths of the gospel, please humor me a bit longer.)

(1) God the Father

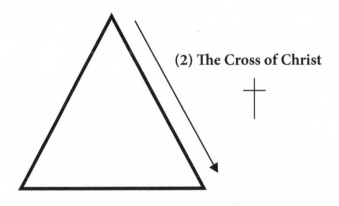

(2) The Cross of Christ

3) Identity

Believing in Jesus Christ and His finished work on the cross affords us a new identity (2 Corinthians 5:17). This identity is God's settled and unchanging disposition to us. Apart from what we do or fail to do, because of the cross, God sees us as holy and dearly loved (Colossians 3:12), righteous (2 Corinthians 5:21), free from condemnation (Romans 8:1), forgiven (1 John 2:2), loved children of God (1 John 3:1), and more. Because of Jesus' death and resurrection, we cannot change how God sees us. His settled and unchanging posture toward us is that we are delighted in (Zephaniah 3:17), complete (Colossians 2:10), servants (1 Corinthians 4:1), and chosen and loved (1 Thessalonians 1:4). Although we are unable to satisfy God's wrath for our sinful, fallen condition, God lovingly provided Jesus as an atoning sacrifice for our sins (1 John 4:10). Jesus Christ, by going to the cross, took what we deserved. He said, "Tetelestai." It is finished. We do not have to do anything to earn our worth or salvation or be more acceptable in God's sight.

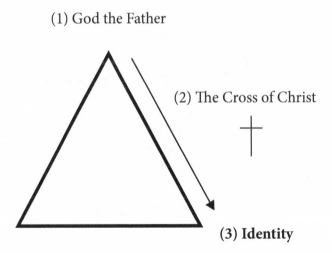

(1) God the Father

(2) The Cross of Christ

(3) **Identity**

4) Submit/Surrender

The only way we can live out of the cross of Christ in our actual lives is to constantly submit and surrender to the finished work of Christ's death and resurrection. As we read earlier, Luther understood this when he said, "The article of justification must be sounded in our ears *incessantly* because the frailty of our flesh will not permit us to take hold of it perfectly and to believe it with all our heart."[20] (italics added, 12). We step more fully into the freedom and abundant living God has for us, not by trying harder to obey, but by constantly submitting and surrendering to God's love and labels. It is not just submitting and surrendering to His forgiveness and love when we sin, but also when we arrogantly believe (under the waterline of awareness, of course) that our good deeds put us in better standing with a perfect and omniscient God to whom "our righteous acts are like filthy rags" (Isaiah 64:6). We must incessantly submit to the identity we have because of Jesus' death and resurrection on our behalf.

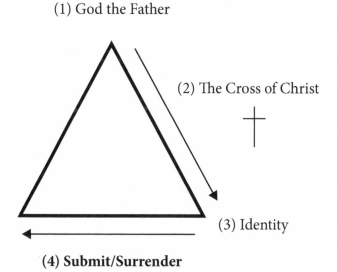

(1) God the Father

(2) The Cross of Christ

(3) Identity

(4) Submit/Surrender

---

[20] (Luther, 2011)

5) Obey/Do

As we continually submit and surrender to who God says we are in Scripture because of Christ's death, a slow but sure shift occurs. As we focus on Christ's grace and forgiveness when we curse, covet our neighbor's new patio set, and despise our in-laws, God's acceptance and love for us because of Jesus organically begins to give us the desire to obey. Obedience is not something we do by trying harder or being more disciplined as much as it is about living out of an overflowing of Christ's love and acceptance for us. There is freedom knowing we are not defined by our actions but by who we are because of Christ's sacrificial death. The more we read God's Word and trust and receive Christ's once-and-for-all forgiveness when we make mistakes, the more we will start to believe and embrace our identity as saints (Colossians 1:2) and children of God (John 1:12). When we start to believe more deeply that we share God's spirit (1 Corinthians 6:17) whether we're acting like a hot mess or Mother Teresa, the more we will step into the *reality* that we are already sanctified by Christ's sacrifice (Hebrews 10:10). The only way God's commands do not feel burdensome (1 John 5:3b) is to continue to "know and have believed the love God has for us" (1 John 4:16a, NASB) over and over and over again in our actual lives.

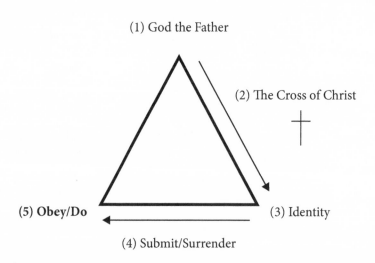

(1) God the Father

(2) The Cross of Christ

(5) Obey/Do

(3) Identity

(4) Submit/Surrender

The Wrong Side of the Triangle

The triangle graphic is pretty straightforward, right? Most of us not only believe the gospel message, but we can recite it inside out and in our sleep. We know we are saved by faith through grace. Like many things hidden deep beneath the surface of our awareness, we assume without question that we believe the gospel message in our core. We quickly dismiss the notion that we could be saved by anything else. We probably are so sure of it, in fact, that we wouldn't need to waste any time paying attention to our ninety percent in this area. However, if we begin to listen to the unintentional, habitual thoughts, behaviors, and actions in our actual lives, we will probably notice some disconnects.

That's what happened to me. Although I knew Scripture and believed that my identity was grounded in God's love and labels for me, I only believed in part. My identity in Christ had not sunk to my core. I was allowing how I looked, that dumb thing I said at my husband's work party, and the fact that I didn't pass college algebra to dictate my worth. Under the waterline of awareness, I felt good about myself (for a moment) if I got a new car, led a Bible study, or someone complimented my outfit. If I watched *The Bachelor* or someone criticized a post I wrote, I was embarrassed and defensive. If someone was unhappy with me, my mind would gravitate relentlessly to what I did or said to upset them. I was consumed by compliments, but I crumbled when I was criticized. As Tim Keller calls it, the penny had not dropped. What I knew about the cross of Christ was an abstraction. I taught and believed it on some level, but it was not operative in my life. What I said, thought, and how I acted gave evidence to what was actually going on in my ninety percent the majority of the time.

I was going down the wrong side of the triangle.

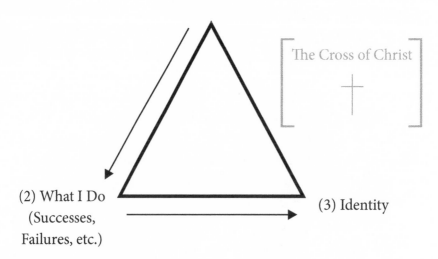

(1) God the Father

The Cross of Christ

(2) What I Do
(Successes,
Failures, etc.)

(3) Identity

Going down the wrong side of the triangle is bypassing the finished work of Christ on the cross. It is focusing and deriving our
identity by our titles and appearance, positive or negative. We go
down the wrong side of the triangle and evade the gospel whenever
we are ashamed or awe-filled by what we do, say, and think. It is
living out of the stress, shame, and "shoulds" of our education, financial situation, obedience, parenting, marriage, awards, and lack
thereof, and finding, under the waterline of awareness, our identity
and worth in what we do or fail to do. It is acknowledging that God
is the Lord of our lives, but that acknowledgment is an abstract belief
that does not impact how we live.

Now What?

Martin Luther said, "You may say, 'The trouble is I don't feel as if I
am righteous.' You must not feel, but believe. Unless you believe that
you are righteous, you do Christ a great wrong, for He has cleansed
you by the washing of regeneration, He died for you so that through

Him you may obtain righteousness and everlasting life."[21] (158). Maybe you identify with the inability to *feel* righteous. Maybe you understand the cross and the triangle illustration, but you do not understand how God sees you as holy and blameless when you do not act that way. Maybe you believe you are fully forgiven and loved, but the more you pay attention to how you respond under the waterline of awareness, you realize that perhaps you believe only in part.

I did not understand how Christ could see me as righteous. I identified with Paul in Romans 7:21-23, "So I find this law at work: Although I want to do good, evil is right there with me. For in my inner being I delight in God's law; but I see another law at work in me, waging war against the law of my mind and making me a prisoner of the law of sin at work within me." I was even more confused by what Paul wrote immediately after that. "Therefore, there is now no condemnation for those who are in Christ Jesus, because through Christ Jesus the law of the Spirit who gives life has set you free from the law of sin and death" (Romans 8:1-2). I cannot tell you how many hours I spent trying to reconcile these two chapters of Scripture.

On the flip side, maybe you do not struggle to feel righteous. Maybe you are like a young woman I'm mentoring named Marcy. Marcy had a 4.0 GPA in high school. She never drank, smoked, or did much of anything wrong. However, Marcy struggles to feel and experience deeply God's love for her. She abstractly knows that Jesus loves her, but she does not believe it in her core. Marcy struggles to reconcile the parable of the vineyard in Matthew 20 where workers who worked for only three hours are paid the same as those who worked all day. She wrestles with the thief on the cross who Jesus welcomes into paradise only because he believed who Jesus was. The more Marcy has struggled to feel God's love and understand passages in the Bible where seemingly lazy or undeserving people are rewarded, the more confused and frustrated she gets.

---

[21] (Luther, 2011)

Isaiah 64:6a says, "All of us have become like one who is unclean, and all our righteous acts are like filthy rags." Going down the wrong side of the triangle is not just about missing the cross of Christ by trying to avoid sin. We can also attempt to bypass the need for Christ's salvation and forgiveness by trying to ensure we don't ever actually need it. Some people are successful; they do not swear or and never had sex outside of marriage. Under the waterline of awareness, "good" Christians can become like the older brother in the story of the prodigal son. Of course, hardly any Protestants would admit or believe they can earn their way to salvation. However, if we have limited tolerance for people who smoke, swear, are atheists, or who we deem to be hypocrites in our ninety percent, we may be going down the wrong side of the triangle too.

The only thing worse than going down the wrong side of the triangle, other than failing to realize that you are in the first place, is not having a clue how to change. I know from experience how disorienting and difficult it is when everything you knew about your faith in Christ is upended. I know how hard it is to realize what you thought were core beliefs are only abstract ones. I empathize and can relate to what Marcy asks me every week when we meet to talk about her inability to experience the freedom of living out of her identity in Christ: "What should I do?"

I wish I could tell Marcy what to do. I wish I could provide a formula or even begin to articulate how we transition from knowing about the cross abstractly to realizing it deeply and living out of the power of Christ's finished work on our behalf. The reason I am unable to answer that question is the indescribable, subtle, but powerful work of the Holy Spirit in us that helps us believe deeper (Titus 3:4-5). Our faith rests on the "power of God" (1 Corinthians 2:5, NASB), and He is the one who teaches us (John 14:26). Although staying connected to the Lord by praying, reading His Word, and being in community with fellow believers in Christ prepares the soil of our hearts for God's work in each of us (1 Corinthians 3:6), we must also grow in reliance upon the Spirit.

What I have told Marcy, however, is that the joy and irony of what she should "do" is that she should stop "doing" altogether. The way we step more fully into and live through the cross of Christ is by shifting our focus away from us and onto knowing and being able to receive God's love and labels for us. We do that by first learning to come down the right side of the triangle and paying attention to when we don't. After that, we focus on submitting and surrendering to the labels God gives us in Scripture, who He says we are because of the cross. Paying attention to and praying about what and if we D.I.B.T., assessing our view of the Lord and learning to enjoy Him, and reading the Bible better by looking for God's love and labels rather than learning what we should do and avoid are all ways to learn to submit and surrender without striving.

Your Turn

Fortunately, there are a few things we can do to ready our hearts and minds for the Spirit's work and prepare the soil of our hearts for rain. This week, pay attention to stress, shame, and shoulds. When you catch yourself thinking, "I *should* have volunteered at the shelter today," or, "I *shouldn't* have watched that movie," make note of it. When you feel shame for being annoyed that your friend is posting pictures of the roses her husband got her "just because," write that down. When you're stressed because you have to complete that project at work or give that presentation, write that down. When you feel amazing because you volunteered at church, take note of that too.

As always, paying attention to the thoughts and feelings floating around in the ninety percent of our brain that we barely hear (or sometimes want to ignore) is not an exercise in shame. We can donate thousands of dollars, win all kinds of awards, and receive excellent test scores and not be going down the wrong side of the triangle. Every motive and thought is not necessarily born out of pride or efforts to bypass the cross of Christ. However, even if they are, the goal of paying attention to the good and bad things we do, say, and think is to help ensure we are filtering everything through the lens of Christ's grace and forgiveness. God, in His love, wants us to pay attention to the good and bad things we do to bypass the cross. Learning to submit and surrender to our identity in Christ, regardless of what we do or how we act, helps free us. When we are trying to achieve or avoid labels that have nothing to do with Christ's free gift of grace, that is a gift to us, so be kind to yourself as you pay attention to your ninety percent.

Write down what you thought or felt when you experienced stress, shame, shoulds, and success. You do not need to justify or explain those feelings. You do not need to describe how you are going to stop doing those things in the future. We will talk about what to do with what you noticed later. Simply pay attention to thoughts like "You should know better," "There you go again," or "That was amazing." And remember, there is no condemnation for you, friend. Jesus already knows and has you covered.

_____

_____

_____

_____

_____

_____

_____

_____

FOR EXAMPLE

What About Me?

One of the most wonderful gifts in my life and ministry is discipling women. The way I learned to disciple like Christ did, however, rarely involves me imparting wisdom or teaching women. More so, it involves listening to them, reflecting back what they say to help them identify what's going on under the waterline of awareness to start replacing abstract beliefs with who God says they are. I feel it is a more effective way of discipling and, best of all, is a very freeing way to walk alongside my sisters in Christ. I don't provide answers or advice. I always say that I simply try to help point women to Christ.

However, after about nine months of walking alongside a young woman in discipleship last year, I realized I was going down the wrong side of the triangle. When Becky was seeking advice for her husband who struggled with substance abuse, I gave her my friend Martha's phone number. Martha was married to an alcoholic and had learned how to listen to her ninety percent. She had for many years prayed for her husband, sought out mentors, and grew in her understanding of her identity in Christ. After Becky called Martha, the following week she had nothing but amazing things to say about Martha. I was thrilled for Becky, until I began to pay attention to my ninety percent while she continued singing Martha's praises. She said Martha had helped her have a major epiphany that turned her thinking and view of herself around. She said Martha was exactly what she needed and was so thankful for the conversation they had.

Although I was nodding and smiling while Becky told me about Martha, under the waterline of awareness I realized I was also jealous. When women in my group would thank me for discipling them,

I would shun those accolades. I believed, in part, that I wasn't doing much, and the Holy Spirit was doing the work. I believed, abstractly, that I could not and did not want credit for any transformation in the lives of those I discipled. However, when I noticed how prickly I was getting as Becky credited Martha with a major turnaround in her life after one conversation, after I had walked alongside Becky for hours every week for almost a year, I knew God had more freedom for me. I did not want to feel jealous and annoyed, but I did. Paying attention to my everyday emotions helped me realize I was craving accolades in my ninety percent. Although that felt somewhat embarrassing to admit, it helped me begin the process of moving abstract beliefs to core ones. Paying attention to the ugly and seemingly petty things under the waterline of awareness is essential. It feels bad, but it is actually amazing because it begins to help us believe deeper.

PART TWO

Now What? How to Transform Faith.

"We begin our Christian life by believing what we are told to believe, then we have to go on to so assimilate our beliefs that they work out in a way that redounds to the glory of God. The danger is in multiplying the acceptation of beliefs we do not make our own."
Oswald Chambers

Week Seven

WHERE YOU REALLY ARE

*"If you wait until your motives are pure and unselfish
before you do something, you will wait forever."*
Tim Keller

When I started paying attention to stress, shame, and shoulds,
I noticed I was going down the wrong side of the triangle in my actual life while perusing social media one day. Over the past several
years, I've volunteered at various nonprofits in the inner city and
at my church, and although I enjoy volunteering, I began to notice,
under the waterline of awareness, that if I saw other volunteers in
pictures and "thank yous" on social media and I wasn't pictured or
thanked, part of me was disappointed. Although I didn't volunteer to
be thanked or tagged, when I wasn't singled out and others were, it
bothered me in my ninety percent. Had I not been in my naked and
afraid discipleship group, I wouldn't have even noticed. However, I
was, and I did. I felt ashamed and embarrassed for being self-centered
and childish, but I began asking the Lord what He wanted me to know
about what I had noticed in surveying my stress, shame, and shoulds.

The more I prayed about why I apparently craved thanks and recognition, the more it happened. I'm a photographer, and whenever I volunteered to photograph a fundraiser or senior photos for families in ministry and I didn't get photo credit when people shared my pictures, I noticed that ugly feeling surfacing again. Instead of getting some great insights into this awful observation when I prayed about it, I simply continued noticing that embarrassing desire in my ninety percent. I was ashamed that I was so petty and needy. I wanted to ignore or fix what was going on in the deep, dark place in my heart and core. However, Patricia kept reminding me in discipleship of something I knew abstractly but struggled to believe in my actual life and embarrassing discoveries: God meets us where we really are.

Jesus' own disciples wanted to sit at His right and left sides in glory (Mark 10:37), and they were jealous of others driving out demons in His name (Mark 9:38-41). In that, Jesus did not scold or chastise his closest followers, but He met them at their places of immaturity and self-centeredness with grace and truth. He met them where they were, not where they should have been. He did not shame them for their desires and real emotions. He did not tell them they "should" know better. Although I knew these passages, I condemned myself for needing validation and thanks. I would beat myself up for serving for selfish reasons. In my ninety percent, I compared myself to others I knew who volunteered humbly and quietly behind the scenes and wondered why I couldn't be more like them.

One of the greatest ironies about the stress, shame, and shoulds we experience is that we wouldn't impose these condemnations or expectations on others. One of my favorite passages to teach when I speak to women is the story of the woman at the well in John 4. I love it because it is a story about Jesus initiating conversation and offering "living water...welling up to eternal life" (John 4:10b, 14b) to a woman who He knew had been married five times and who felt undeserving. I love that He offers the woman His grace and acceptance before she repented or fully understood who He was. I enjoy reminding women that Jesus lovingly met the woman in the midst of her shame and defensiveness, but ironically, I resisted letting Him meet me in mine.

We can believe deeply and in our core the message of the cross of Christ for others, but under the waterline of awareness, we often personally bypass and believe it abstractly for ourselves. Recognizing the stress, shame, and shoulds buried deeply in our ninety percent can start to expose those disconnects, though. Reminding ourselves that the Lord meets us with love and acceptance in our real doubts and partial beliefs can make us more willing and able to ask Him for help in the places where we are going down the wrong side of the triangle in our actual lives. After all, if I believed in my core that God loved and accepted me whether I was scouring social media to see if I was in a group photo or not, why would I feel so ashamed and embarrassed about doing exactly that?

God Meets Us Where We Really Are

Scripture affirms that God meets us where we are, including and typically in the mundane parts of our lives. Just as Jesus met the woman at the well she probably visited every day for most of her adult life, He appeared to Moses in a burning bush while he was tending sheep (Exodus 3:4) and met Abraham at the door of the tent where he lived (Genesis 18:1). He met Jacob where he had stopped on a trip because he was tired (Genesis 32:1-2), and Jesus helped Peter catch fish while he worked tirelessly to earn a living on his boat (Luke 5:1-11). Jesus met Nathaniel under a fig tree (John 1:43-51), and the Holy Spirit gave Philip directions while he was traveling along a desert road (Acts 8:26). Often, we expect the Lord to meet us through magnificent people and monumental places, but Scripture reminds us that God meets people most often in the ordinary and obscure.

Scripture also says that since the Holy Spirit lives in every believer of Jesus Christ (Romans 8:11) and that God is always at work (John 5:17), God also meets us where we really are in the depths of our hearts and minds. He meets us in our deep thoughts (1 Corinthians 2:12-16) and in discerning our beliefs about God (Ephesians 1:17). David took his real emotions and struggles to the Lord (Psalms 5:1-3, 13:1-3, 43:5), as did Habakkuk with his complaints and questions (Habakkuk 1, 2). He meets us when we struggle with anxiety (Philippians 4:6-7, 1 Peter 5:7), and He meets us without condemnation to help us realize—in our actual desires and emotions—the freedom and abundant life He came to give us through Jesus Christ (John 10:10).

Your Turn

This week, take some time to evaluate your everyday emotions in your actual life. What conversations this week annoyed you? What person at work repeatedly brought you joy? Who brought you angst? When were you jealous or defensive with your spouse? Write down what you notice. Circle the *one* emotion or physical response you *repeatedly* experienced in dealing with people and situations this week in your actual life. If it is hard to decide which one to circle, select the one you would be most thrilled to rid yourself of.

Emotions are God-given. Evaluating our everyday emotions can help expose fears and abstract beliefs under the waterline of our awareness. Emotions can be wonderful guides, but they are not a means to govern our lives or cover us with guilt. Assigning shoulds and shame to the real emotions the Lord has given us is not helpful or productive. As you circle a difficult or recurring emotion, do not attempt to solve or justify it. Ask the Lord to help you live out of Christ's love and grace for you when you experience or respond out of this emotion. If you must do something with what you noticed this week, ask God what He wants you to know about your anger or propensity to talk unkindly about yourself. Continue praying about your everyday emotion and listen for anything you sense the Lord may be revealing to you during your time in His Word and in prayer.

_____

_____

_____

_____

_____

_____

_____

_____

_____

_____

_____

_____

_____

_____

_____

_____

_____

_____

_____

_____

_____

FOR EXAMPLE

The Selfie

Last December, about a month after my biking accident, I took a selfie with my son Casey. A local mom who had lost her eight-year-old son, Jacob, had asked his classmates to wear their baseball jerseys to school to honor Jacob, who loved the game. The request went viral, and everyone from professional baseball players to newscasters were sharing Jacob's mom's request so everyone could join in supporting his family. Casey and I had donned our jerseys that Friday afternoon, so we took a selfie together. Well, we actually took three selfies…

Just two days before I took my selfie, I had cried while praying with some friends for Jacob's mom and family. For weeks I had been praying for this family after hearing about Jacob, and I wanted to share our picture using Jacob's hashtag because his mom was making an album of all the photos of people wearing their jerseys to give to her son's baseball team. I wanted to do something for this family, but I could barely walk across the room without help. I wanted to support a grieving mother, and this was a small way I could. Although my motives started out pure and right, they did not end there.

After I took the selfie of Casey and I, I didn't like how it looked, so I took it again. I still thought I looked terrible, even after adding a filter, so I took it a third time. Finally, my son assured me I looked fine and reminded me kindly, "It's for Jacob, Mom." After continuing to edit one of the three photos and posting it on social media, I was overcome with embarrassment. Under the waterline of awareness, I began to berate myself. "Who takes a picture for a family who tragically lost their eight-year-old son and makes it about themself? Who is so preoccupied with their looks that they obsess about a picture

meant to honor someone and support their grieving family? I wonder if anyone else's adult son had to remind them the purpose of
Jacob's selfie." I felt very embarrassed and ashamed about that selfie
until I finally heard what was going on in my ninety percent and
reminded myself that the Lord would never talk to me like I was
talking to myself.

God meets us where we really are, and where I really was was
broken. Using a walker and having a knee the size of a cantaloupe
did not make me feel particularly attractive. Although perhaps I
shouldn't have cared about that, I did. I cared about it before I broke
my leg too, but using a walker made me even more self-conscious.
As I began to evaluate my everyday emotions, I realized the Lord
was not on His throne rolling His eyes at the fact that I had made
Jacob's selfie about me. I remembered Psalms 103:8: "The Lord is
compassionate and gracious, slow to anger and abounding in love." I
reminded myself in my shame that God meets us where we really are
without condemning us or beating us up. In doing so, as we submit
and surrender to who He says we are, regardless of our preoccupation with our looks, education, and finances, we begin to care a little
less about those things that exhaust and distract us from the cross of
Christ in the first place.

Week Eight

ASKING THE OBVIOUS

*"So they called to the blind man, 'Cheer up! On your feet! He's call-
ing you.' Throwing his cloak aside, he jumped to his feet and came to
Jesus. 'What do you want me to do for you?' Jesus asked him."*
Mark 10:49b-51a

He was called Blind Bartimaeus. Everyone in Jericho would have
probably recognized the "son of Timaeus" since he was always along
the roadside begging. Surely Jesus knew. Jesus, who was fully God
and fully man, knew what was unseen, unsaid, and undercover. He
knew what people were thinking (Mark 2:8) and if their motives
were good or not (John 2:25). Jesus knew everything about the lives
of those he encountered (John 4:17-19), yet He always asked people
questions, even when the question and its answer seemed obvious.

- To a blind man asking Jesus for healing, "What do you want
  me to do for you?" (Matthew 20:32)
- To the apostles in a storm on the sea, "Why are you afraid?"
  (Matthew 8:26)

- To the father with the demon-possessed son, "How long has he been like this?" (Mark 9:21)
- To a woman who touched Jesus' robe for healing, "Who touched my clothes?" (Mark 5:30)
- To a woman caught in adultery, "Woman, where are they? Has no one condemned you?" (John 8:10)

Jesus often confronted His listeners "with their own thought process, preconceptions, assumptions, and beliefs."[22] It seemed, based on His questions, that Jesus used them to help people get below the waterline of their own awareness. He frequently used questions to hold up a mirror for people to see what they only believed in part to help them believe deeper. Perhaps Jesus, in His love, asked questions to help people move their abstract beliefs about Him, and what their belief in Him afforded them in their actual lives, down into their bones.

Before Jesus healed a man who had been an invalid for thirty-eight years, He again asked a seemingly obvious question, "Do you want to get well?" (John 5:6b). What was the impetus for Jesus' question? Perhaps the beggar who frequented the healing pool only abstractly thought he wanted to be well. Maybe, in his core, it was frightening to consider a life where he, possibly for the first time, did not have to depend on others for help. Maybe the predictability of life and his infirmity had become safe and even emotionally and mentally comfortable. Could it be that Jesus asked what seemed like obvious questions because He knew that sometimes the thought of changing—no matter how debilitating and unappealing our current state of existence may be—is often more frightening than staying the same?

In his book *The Rest of God*, Mark Buchanan said, "Change begins with fresh eyes, in other words. It begins with an awakened

---

[22] (Sternke, Tebbe, 2016)

imagination. You turn away, stubbornly and without apology, from that which formerly entranced you, and you turn toward that which once you avoided. You start to see what God sees, and as God sees it"[23] (5). Perhaps Jesus asked questions to help his hearers identify what entranced them. He certainly would have known that to turn away from something and toward an unknown but seemingly desirable something else isn't obvious or something we do easily. Jesus, fully man and fully God, understood the human condition, that oftentimes we know what we hate about our current reality but don't have the faintest idea how to live differently. Questions can help change that. Jesus knew the power of questions in exposing doubt and awakening our imagination to the more He has for everyone who believes in Him.

The Power of Why

When I realized, under the waterline of awareness, that I wanted to be tagged and given photo credit, I began to do what Jesus did. I asked myself a seemingly obvious question: Why? *Why* did I want to be seen and thanked? *Why* was that significant to me? When I began asking why, I quickly defaulted to wanting to explain or ignore where I really was. Rather than ask why I wanted attention and praise with the grace and compassion Jesus did, I went down the wrong side of the triangle. I wanted to explain my sophomoric emotions. I wanted to justify why I felt the way I did. I did not want to spend time asking why for these embarrassing admissions.

Eventually, however, in my discipleship group and with Patricia's help, I was able to merely ask why without condemning myself. I was able to go down the wrong side of the triangle less. Patricia reminded me time and time again that God had freedom for me. My identity was not in being a selfless volunteer, nor was it in embarrassment of wishing people would thank me for helping, but that God's disposi-

---

[23] (Buchanan, 2006)

tion and heart for me were unchanging because of Christ's sacrifice on the cross. She helped me remember to go down the right side of the triangle as I asked why.

Gradually, I began to step further toward this difficult question. I would ask myself, patiently and more compassionately, why it was meaningful for me to be seen and appreciated. My first thought was "Doesn't everybody?" As I prayed about that question for a few days, the Lord reminded me of several people that did not care about those things. My husband and my best friend both hate attention and, unlike me, do not seem to be annoyed when they aren't recognized or singled out. As I continued to pray about why it was meaningful for me to be seen and thanked, I realized that even if other people did have these desires, for me it was a source of exhaustion and preoccupation that I detested. Being seen and appreciated was a place of bondage that *I* wanted freedom from, so I needed to go deeper.

I continued asking why. Why *did* I want to be thanked and recognized? Why was it so mentally and emotionally consuming when I was not appreciated or in the spotlight? After spending many days and weeks thinking and praying about this question, I came to the conclusion that being thanked and recognized made me feel good. This gross, selfish thought felt more embarrassing and awful than acknowledging that I wanted recognition in the first place, but asking why is not supposed to feel amazing. Getting freed from captivity rarely does.

Every answer to why led me to another why. In order to move to places of deeper belief and transformation in our faith and actual lives, we must peel back layers. We must go deeper. We must bravely practice asking and praying about why over and over and over again. Why did being thanked and recognized feel good? Once again, my temptation was to give up or fix my problem by reverting to vague responses that evaded where I actually was. But answers like "Doesn't it feel good for everyone?" do not lead to freedom because they do not meet me where I really am. They do not address my actual wants and emotions. So, as petty and ridiculous as it felt to ask why again, I spent some more time thinking and asking the Lord why feeling good about other people thanking and recognizing me is something I crave. The process of exposing doubt and transforming my faith is difficult and slow, but persisting in the difficult process of asking why is how we get well.

Your Turn

What repeated or difficult emotion or response did you circle in the last chapter? Did you notice you were often jealous of others? Did you realize you were often angry at your children or spouse? Did you find your know-it-all coworkers annoying multiple days in a row? One of the ways we can get beneath the waterline of awareness to unearth abstract beliefs is to ask ourselves, "Why?" Why did you beat yourself up when you burned dinner? Why did your mother-in-law's comment upset you? Why do you tend to avoid people who are too quiet, direct, or evasive?

As it did in Scripture, "Why?" seems like an obvious question, but do not give up going deeper. God has more for you. Ask why of your real emotions and responses without shaming or "shoulding" yourself. Meet yourself with compassion and love as Jesus did, where you really are. When you courageously start to pray about and respond to the whys you are asking, continue asking why some more. Emotions should not control us, but God gave them to us to consider. Evaluating our emotions through prayer, time in the Word, and Christian community can help us identify and strip back layers of abstract beliefs we have about the Lord, beliefs that impact our unintentional, habitual thoughts, behaviors, and actions. God has more freedom for you, so don't give up! Keep paying attention with the love and compassion Christ has for you.

_____

_____

_____

_____

_____

_____

_____

_____

_____

_____

_____

_____

_____

_____

_____

_____

_____

_____

_____

_____

_____

_____

_____

_____

_____

_____

_____

_____

_____

_____

_____

_____

_____

_____

_____

_____

_____

_____

_____

_____

_____

_____

_____

_____

_____

_____

_____

FOR EXAMPLE

Five-Cent Soup Packs

Recently, I had to go with my husband to a meeting with a financial planner. I'm married to an engineer who is the senior vice president of supply chain for a large company. When I was twenty-eight years old, I left my teaching career to become a stay-at-home mom. Once our children were in middle school, I started and have continued working in ministry. My contribution to our income is negligible, and abstractly, I don't care about that. I wanted to stay home, and I love serving in ministry; both have been a gift and privilege. However, before we left for the financial planning meeting, I noticed something going on under the waterline of my awareness. I was angsty.

When I realized that, I began to ask why. Why was I dreading going, and why did I keep asking Chris if I *had* to go along? Well, for one thing, I'm terrible at math. I hate numbers, and the part of my brain that is supposed to know how to understand decimal points, time zones, and algebra is broken or at some point fell out of my head. Additionally, I don't know what a portfolio is or why it needs to be managed. Nor do I really care. Why does my hatred of math and disinterest of investing make me nervous for a meeting where Chris assured me I wouldn't have to say much if I didn't want to? As I continued to pay attention and ask why, I realized there was a lot going on under the waterline of awareness that was making me anxious.

I did not like seeing what I earned annually on paper, especially next to what my husband made. I was worried the financial planner would think I was lazy, dumb, or both. I also did not want to be asked questions at the meeting that I might not be able to answer. Part of me was also embarrassed that I buy my husband Valentine's and birthday gifts with money I did not earn. The more I asked why, the more horrible things I found lurking around in my ninety percent.

It is difficult for me to write these embarrassing thoughts on paper. It is hard to admit that these things bother me. Some of you are thinking I shouldn't let them bother me. If you were here, you might tell me, "Who cares what people think?" However, if this is where I *really* am and how I *really* feel, someone telling me that I shouldn't feel that way or that I should quit feeling that way does not help me, at least not deeply. Getting further down to the root of why those thoughts and perceptions bother me, on the other hand, just might. So, I spent some time asking another obvious question: Why *did* those things bother me?

Although Chris would never and has never made me feel as if I wasn't doing or making "enough," I grew up paying for everything myself. I bought my own car and have paid for my own gas and car insurance since I was old enough to drive. I paid my own way through college while also paying for everything from my rent to ramen noodles in bulk. Although supporting myself was expected and necessary, doing so had evolved into going down the wrong side of the triangle without me realizing it. I used to feel good about my ability to support myself. I was proud that I had paid my own way through college. In my ninety percent, I think I felt safer and more significant when I was a high school teacher before becoming a stay-at-home mom. Somewhere along the line, what I earned had gotten tangled up in what I was worth.

How did I get from feeling a little restless about going to a meeting to realizing I had been going down the wrong side of the triangle with my successes and failures for many years? By asking why of my hidden, difficult thoughts over and over again, I was able to identify what was going on in my ninety percent. Doing so allowed me to peel back layers and expose disconnects that I was able to take to the Lord in prayer. It also moved me closer toward trusting and believing more deeply who He says I am, regardless of my annual salary or inability to balance a checkbook.

Week Nine

HUGGING YOUR CACTUS

"I remember my affliction and my wandering, the bitterness and the gall. I well remember them, and my soul is downcast within me. Yet this I call to mind and therefore I have hope: Because of the Lord's great love we are not consumed, for his compassions never fail. They are new every morning; great is your faithfulness. I say to myself, 'The Lord is my portion; therefore, I will wait for him.'"
Lamentations 3:19-24

I remember driving to my discipleship group one day, about six months into learning how to pay attention to my actual life, when I was overcome with rage. I swore out loud when a car cut me off, and I contemplated turning around and going home. I did not want to talk to my discipleship group about what I was noticing. It was embarrassing to share my answers to "why" and what felt like pointless observations. Although I understood abstractly that asking why was meant to help me pay attention and not pinpoint an answer, what I really wanted was a single epiphany to help me move on with my life. I knew God would meet me where I was and that I was going down the wrong side of the triangle, but I didn't care. However, as I confessed all of this angrily to Patricia when I arrived to Season 1, Episode 27 of *Naked and Afraid*, she just smiled and nodded calmly. She seemed almost happy that I was having a mental and emotional breakdown. She said I was doing a great job and that part of the process of paying attention was "hugging my cactus."

Hugging one's cactus is prayerfully and intentionally choosing to sit in the uncomfortable spaces of actively paying attention and listening to the Lord. It is holding on to what's prickly and difficult. It is asking why over and over again to peel back layers of awareness. It is becoming mindful of abstract versus core beliefs, and it's doing it all without trying to fix or control. If it were more fun, we would call it "hugging a puppy," but the thorny and unpleasant process of waiting on the Lord is worth it. Hugging our cactus and repeatedly asking why helps us begin to believe deeper. Waiting on the Lord and paying attention to our emotions unearths abstract beliefs and helps us move toward the freedom God has for us, but doing so rarely feels good.

Learning to Unlearn

If praying about and asking why of recurring everyday emotions and unintentional thoughts, behaviors, and actions feels like hugging a cactus, why do it? Part of moving to deeper places of belief and transformation is not only learning to identify abstract beliefs but dismantling them. The tracks we have gone down for decades are deep. Going down the wrong side of the triangle has been our pattern for a long time. In order to begin to make new tracks, we need to take apart the old ones. We have to debunk old, longstanding lies and abstract beliefs. As I heard someone say recently, "Often we have a lot of unlearning to do before we can learn something new." Hugging our cactus and asking why of our everyday emotions helps us take to God that which we need to prayerfully and, in a posture of submission, unlearn.

One of the things I needed to unlearn was defaulting to fast fixes when I was uncomfortable or struggling. The more I asked the Lord what He wanted me to know about my desire to be seen and thanked, the more He allowed me to see how exhausting and prevalent those desires were. Rather than having an aha moment while reading my Bible or fasting, I noticed that I was checking my social media page for "likes" *again*. I realized that I felt elated if I was asked to speak at a women's event but questioned my abilities if they never invited me back again. I caught myself looking for something annoying or wrong with successful, polished women I interfaced with. Part of hugging your cactus is simply becoming more and more aware of how frequent and tiring the recurring everyday emotions that we wish would go away are in our lives.

Waiting on the Lord also feels like hugging a cactus because embarrassment, frustration, and shame seem to crop up constantly while we wait. It is hard to go down the right side of the triangle and remember that God's disposition to us is settled and unchanging because of the cross when we are noticing seemingly childish and superficial things about ourselves over and over again. Staying present in what the Lord is spotlighting to us *in His love* without feeling shameful is something we need to ask the Lord to help us do. Memorizing Lamentations 3:19-24 has also helped me focus on the Lord and His sovereignty in my cactus hugging, as did talking to other Christian friends who did not try to transplant or kill my cactus. Hugging our cactus and learning and practicing waiting on the Lord, though painful, helps ensure we do not return as soon or as often to those old tracks of condemnation.

Although hugging our cactus does not feel efficient or productive, it helps to remember that we are *actively* waiting. When we ask the Lord what He wants us to know about our recurring everyday emotions, we are looking. We are paying attention as we read Scripture and pray, "Spirit, help me see." We are looking for God to meet us where we really are, and as we wait, we are continuing to prayer-fully ask why as we pay attention to what's going on in our ninety percent. We are hugging our cactus to continue to move toward something a friend reminded me of when we were talking about how mentally and emotionally exhausting transformation was. I told her I did not like looking beneath the waterline of awareness because it is so dark and frightening to uncover. I added that this process was depressing and often frustrating, and although she agreed, my sweet friend Mindy stopped, looked me square in the eyes with genuine compassion and love, and asked me, "But don't you want to be free?"

Harboring animosity when I am not thanked or given photo credit does not feel like freedom. It is exhausting to try to ensure that people think my motives are good. It is frustrating to wish I wouldn't care if I receive photo credit, and I would probably say I don't care, but based on my everyday thoughts and responses, it's obvious I do care. Recurring everyday emotions feel exactly like what they are: bondage. Being consumed by many of these emotions robs me of the ability to be present with the people in front of me. As we go through the inefficient and sometimes painful process of asking and answer-ing why of our recurring everyday emotions, we must remember the goal. We are trying to create room in our heart and imagination for the more God has for us. As you ask why of your anger, jealousy, or inability to receive compliments and you want to quit or throw up, maybe asking yourself my friend's honest question will help you per-severe. Don't you want to be free?

Your Turn

This week, continue asking why of the everyday recurring emo-tion you circled in Chapter Eight. If you were able to answer some whys in the last chapter, continue asking why of what you unearthed. Hug your cactus. Perhaps you noticed conversations, relationships, or more emotions that coincided with what you have been asking the

Lord about. What Scriptures are you reading that address or challenge that recurring emotion or help you move deeper into the why underneath it? Write down anything you notice and continue hugging your cactus. God has freedom for you as you do so. Keep asking Him what He wants you to know about this thorny subject.

As always, be nice to yourself in this process! The Lord would not tell you to just quit feeling jealous or defensive. He wouldn't call you immature or a bad Christian. In fact, there's no such thing as a bad Christian. Scripture says that if we trust in Jesus' death and resurrection, He has become for us our "righteousness, holiness, and redemption" (1 Corinthians 1:30b). God does not, because of Jesus, count our sins against us (2 Corinthians 5:19b). One of the only ways we can be a "bad Christian," based on what the Bible says, is to go down the wrong side of the triangle and bypass the cross of Christ altogether.

_____

_____

_____

_____

_____

_____

_____

_____

_____

_____

_____

_____

_____

_____

_____

_____

_____

_____

_____

_____

_____

_____

_____

_____

_____

_____

_____

_____

_____

_____

_____

_____

_____

_____

FOR EXAMPLE

Needing to be Needed

Kate didn't know why she let her family down, again. She told her husband she would help clean out the garage, but when a friend called her and asked if they could talk, Kate went to meet her for coffee instead. When her conversation with her friend went longer than expected, she felt guilty she had not gotten home sooner. Kate knew her husband and children would understand, and they did, but she also felt she was taking advantage of them.

During our discipleship group, I asked Kate a seemingly obvious question: Why did she feel like she was taking advantage of her family? I knew Kate pretty well. I could not imagine her taking advantage of anyone intentionally, nor could I imagine her saying that of anyone else. When we say things about ourselves that we would not say about someone else, that is a pretty good indicator that we are condemning ourselves. Kate said she felt like she was taking advantage of her family because although they had needed her too, she had chosen to be with her friend longer than she should have. She also said she felt that way because she's made her family wait for her before.

When I asked Kate what it does in and for her to be there for friends, even though it seems to lead to her feeling guilty afterwards, she realized something significant going on in her ninety percent. "I think it feels better to be needed by people *outside* my family." When I asked her why, she paused for a very long time. "I don't know." We decided that might be a good question to ask the Lord about until we met again for our discipleship group.

However, the next week at discipleship, Kate still was not quite sure why it felt good to be needed. The only thing she noticed as she prayed the previous week were more opportunities to help people outside her family, and one of those opportunities resulted in her helping someone and making her family wait for her, *again*. As she shared all of this with some obvious frustration and disappointment, I got the same smile on my face that my friend had when I was angrily swearing on my way to my discipleship group. Kate was exactly where she was supposed to be. She was hugging her cactus.

The following week, Kate began to pay attention to some other things the Lord was showing her. She came back and shared some more difficult things that she was able to continue asking why about. Through those questions, she arrived at some bad news she was believing about herself and some abstract beliefs she had about the Lord in that bad news. Kate gave herself grace as she clung onto that which was prickly and embarrassing. In her cactus hugging, she dug deeper and discovered things below the waterline of awareness that had been keeping her from the freedom God, in His love, had for her and has for each one of us.

Week Ten

QUICK FIXES

"Jesus looked at him and loved him. 'One thing you lack,' he said. 'Go and sell everything you have and give to the poor, and you will have treasure in heaven. Then come, follow me.' At this the man's face fell. He went away sad, because he had great wealth."
Mark 10:21-22

One of the things I've noticed about women, in particular, is we like helping others. We like to problem-solve and make everything better. Most women I know, myself included, love to help and encourage our friends, sisters, and even random strangers. We love affirming other women's intelligence, inner and outer beauty, and how amazing their outfit looks. Edifying others can be a wonderful thing, but like many good things, there can be a shadow side to our propensity to counsel and compliment that unfortunately isn't helpful when it comes to identifying the lies we believe and turning abstract beliefs into core ones.

There can be several negative by-products in trying to help people feel better. One shadow side to providing others with fast solutions to their problems is that sometimes quick fixes can be about us. Sometimes, like Kate, helping others makes us feel smart and needed, but under the waterline of awareness, we are hoping they will take our advice. Sometimes, we are providing solutions in order to manage outcomes, like when I share my wise, unsolicited advice with one of my adult children. The unfortunate irony and by-product of our attempts to fix and control, however, can be getting ahead of the Holy Spirit and potentially delaying God's good and perfect plan and purpose.

If we look to Jesus as our example, He did not always fix people's problems. In the story of the wealthy young ruler in Mark 10, we see that although Jesus loved the man, He let him walk away sad. Jesus did not try to convince or chase after the man. He didn't reframe or soften what He told the man either. He ultimately held up a mirror to the young ruler and helped him see that his love and priorities would ultimately fail to satisfy or save him apart from first loving and trusting Jesus deeply. Jesus allowed the man to hug his cactus, and He did not fix anything or control outcomes. Jesus did not feel bad or better about Himself because people took or failed to take His advice. Jesus was one with the Father and helped create the universe, yet even He often did not solve people's problems for them.

Get Over It Already

As I continued paying attention to and asking why it felt good to be recognized and appreciated, I often grew tired and annoyed with hugging my cactus, so I would revert to quick fixes. I would tell myself that I shouldn't care if people thanked me because I knew they were grateful. I read and journaled verses like Galatians 1:10a, "For am I now seeking the approval of man, or of God?", and Matthew 6:1a, "Be careful not to practice your righteousness in front of others to be seen by them." However, that usually made me feel more embarrassed and ashamed. I continued trying to quickly fix my problem. Sometimes that looked like ignoring it and hoping it would go away. Sometimes it looked like telling myself to grow up. But the problem with quick and easy fixes is that they lack effectiveness. Even if I temporarily felt better by telling myself to get over it or by memorizing a verse, the next time I felt ignored or unappreciated, the cycle would begin again.

Matt Chandler said, "Grace-driven effort wants to get to the bottom of behavior, not just manage behavior. If you're simply managing behavior but not removing the roots of that behavior, then the weeds simply sprout up in another place"[24] (214). The problem with quick fixes or memorizing Scripture we only believe in part to quickly address our real emotions and struggles is that we are not getting to the root of the problem. If we cannot hug our cactus and sit in the difficult places where the Lord in His love wants us to believe deeper, we will not be moved to transformation in our actual lives. Often when I walk alongside women in discipleship, rather than hugging their cactus by asking why and waiting on the Lord, they often instead default to problem-solving.

One woman in my discipleship group was struggling with her high school senior's college and career choices. Rather than asking herself why her son's choices were upsetting, she went into fix-it and condemnation mode, saying, "I just need to pray for discernment." Another woman was struggling with feeling exhausted by ministry. When I asked her why she was tired, she responded curtly, "I just don't trust God enough. I need to remember He is in control." Another young woman was trying to figure out if a guy she was dating was God's best for her, but instead of answering what she meant by "God's best" and what that would look like, she told me, "I just have to quit thinking about it so much." All of these things manage behavior. They are not necessarily bad or untrue, but as Chandler observed above, until the root of whatever ails us is addressed, the

---

[24] (Chandler, 2012)

problem is not gone. It is, at best, hidden and waiting to resurface in another place.

Your Turn

So, what do we do instead of trying to quickly fix what ails us? What do we do instead of trying to place bandages on deep, lifelong lacerations? We continue to ask why. We have to hug our cactus and remember to give ourselves the time, vision, and grace Jesus always gave people. We must continue asking the Lord what He wants us to know about our everyday emotions, why we feel threatened, angry, or apathetic, then look for Scripture to encourage and teach us. We must continue prayerfully examining our relationships and responses without trying to pretty them up. We can also seek out wise Christian sisters who will listen without fixing or giving quick solutions and who will pray for and encourage us as we hug our cactus.

Asking why and praying about the same things can be annoying and frustrating, but doing so helps peel back layers of lies and abstract beliefs that we've believed for years. Lies and beliefs that are not in line with what God says about you. If you are frustrated with what you've been noticing in the past two weeks, tell the Lord that too. He can handle it and could not be more in love with you. Remember that you did not get here overnight. As you continue to patiently and prayerfully ask why, write down anything you notice. Look in Scripture and continue asking the Father what else He wants to show you in this struggle. As you wait and listen, write down what the Lord seems to be showing you in His Word and in your actual life. In His love, He wants to help you find more freedom. He wants you to learn to wait and look for Him patiently in the more He has for you.

_____

_____

FOR EXAMPLE

In Control

Sandy was a sweet, put-together woman. In discipleship, she did an excellent job of paying attention to her ninety percent, and she had great examples of relationships and abstract beliefs she was wrestling. Unlike me, Sandy would come back to group each week and seem to have tidy, concrete solutions to whatever she was asking the Lord about. Whenever I asked the Lord why I felt panicked when someone disagreed with me on social media or what He wanted me to know about why I was nervous about an upcoming family get-to-gether, it took me weeks and months to get to any sort of convoluted sense of an epiphany or deeper awareness. I felt like I must not be as good at hearing from the Lord, or that I did not have a faith as deep as Sandy's.

However, one week, Sandy got upset. She said she did not like asking why, paying attention to her ninety percent, or hugging her proverbial cactus. She was annoyed and frustrated by our disciple-ship group, not because she felt naked and afraid, but for the first time since our group began, Sandy could not quickly fix a situation in her actual life. She couldn't control this complicated problem, or the painful feelings associated with it, and the inability to do either became overwhelming.

Eventually, Sandy was able to start asking why without fixing or trying to control difficult situations and relationships. She was able to hug her cactus. She realized the freedom that comes when we ac-cept in our core, that we do not have control and that we cannot rush through the places the Lord, in His love, wants to take us. In that place, Sandy was able to expose doubt and believe deeper more quickly and easily. She was able to submit and surrender to the Lord's love and labels more easily too. Fast fixes can often be the result of going down the wrong side of the triangle. We can equate our ability to problem-solve or quickly control anything that is painful and messy with our identity and worth. However, the safer and more loved and accepted Sandy felt by the Lord despite her inability to fix and control her life, the more she was able to depend on the cross for her identity and worth.

Week Eleven

LEANING INTO GOD'S LOVE AND LABELS

*"An obedient person is someone who can listen to
the voice of Him who calls him the beloved."*
Henri Nouwen[25]

I am incredibly passionate about the concepts in this book. I have walked alongside many women in an effort to help them pay attention to their unintentional habits, thoughts, behaviors, and actions. Although I love speaking at conferences and retreats, I also enjoy discipling women in weekly small groups to help them expose abstract beliefs and make new tracks. I love teaching women about going down the right side of the triangle because I personally lived too long with the disconnect between what I knew about God and the Bible and experiencing Him and His truths in my actual life. Why should we hug our cactus and try to quit ignoring and fixing all that we want to change about ourselves? Why go through all of this and accept that this process never ends? Because until we identify abstract beliefs and continually move what we know about God and

---

[25] (Nouwen, 1992)

the Bible from our head and into our hearts more and more, I believe it will be difficult to realize the abundant freedom, joy, and peace God has for us through Christ's death and resurrection.

After many months of hugging my cactus and asking why it felt good to be thanked and recognized, the Lord revealed several things going on in my ninety percent. The Spirit helped me realize I was looking for my identity in the opinions of others. Like the young high school girl I walked alongside in discipleship, the Lord showed me that I was almost constantly condemning myself in the process. Ultimately, almost if not all of our issues and unrealized areas of faith stem from an identity crisis. Although we believe in part that we are daughters of the King and our worth is settled, many of us have a fragile sense of worth and confidence in the Lord and in ourselves when it comes to our actual lives.

What do we do after we continually ask the Lord what He wants us to know about our everyday emotions? What do we do when we discover partial and abstract beliefs or that we are going down the wrong side of the triangle? After we ask the Lord what He wants us to know about the "whys" we detest and struggle with repeatedly, how do we move to places of greater freedom and abundant living? As we continue to remind ourselves that God is kind and compassionate and abounding in love (Psalms 103:8-12) and as we hug our cactus in the dark and difficult areas of our ninety percent that are infiltrating our lives, we need to continue staying connected to the Vine. We need to continually return to God's Word, be reminded of the love and labels He has for us and move personally and intimately toward experiencing the fact that He calls us beloved, equipped, and complete in Christ. As David and others did in the Psalms, we remember and recite God's loving character and protection in the midst of our real struggles and doubts (3:5-6, 17:7, 33:20-22, 41:9-12, 43:5, 44:26, 70:4-5, 107:13-15).

Let My Vindication Come From You

After weeks and months of prayerfully paying attention as I read God's Word and talking with my trusted friend and mentor about why I cared so much about what others thought of me, I decided to start a list in my journal of who God says I am because of Jesus' death and resurrection. This is the list I started:

- I'm made in God's image and likeness (Genesis 1:26)
- I'm loved and accepted (Luke 15:11-32)
- I'm valuable (Luke 15:8-10)
- I'm the salt of the earth (Matthew 5:13)
- I'm the light of the world (Matthew 5:14)
- I'm forgiven (Ephesians 4:32)
- I'm a child of God (John 1:12)

These and other verses I have since added to the list of who God says I am define me. The real or imagined judgmental glances of others do not define me. My salary, intelligence, and looks (good, bad, or otherwise) do not define me. The names I call myself and the motives I sometimes assign what I do also do not define me. As I have looked more closely at and interrogated my beliefs about God's disposition toward me, I have been learning to do for the first time what I hadn't been able to do before asking questions and hugging my cactus: trust more deeply that who God says I am matters more than my opinion or the opinion of those around me.

It was not that I had never seen these verses before. I had read hundreds of times that I was fearfully and wonderfully made and that God delighted over me with singing. I knew that He knew the number of hairs on my head. However, I also knew that I did not trust God in my core to protect my kids, to fully accept the complicated parts of me, or that His opinion was more significant than what someone said about me in the past. Until I began examining my ninety percent, I did not know how often I was going down the wrong side of the triangle. I did not realize my view of the Father was skewed. Until I learned how to examine what was going on under the waterline of awareness without shoulds, shame, and condemnation, I did not know how to step into deeper belief or transformation. I believed all of these verses for my daughters, best friend, and the hundreds of women I've spoken to over the years, but I did not realize I did not deeply believe them for myself.

So, Now What?

When I first started writing this book, I wanted to call it *But How?* Most of what we feel we are missing in our faith does not stem from a lack of knowing what we need to do but how to implement those things in a meaningful way. One practical thing that is helping me step closer to the Lord's love and labels for me is pondering and personalizing pertinent passages about who Christ says I am. (Sorry, I'm a former special education teacher. I love alliterations.)

Pondering a verse means reading and thinking about it many times for many days. Pondering Scripture is praying over and questioning it until you sense the Lord has revealed everything He wants to show you in it. It is embracing and welcoming that dreaded and inefficient pace we began our journey with: "slow." It is memorizing God's Word in order to hide it in your heart (Psalms 119:11) and guard your course (Proverbs 2:8). Committing Scripture verses to memory is a practical and powerful way to take lies and abstract beliefs captive and make them obedient to Christ (2 Corinthians 10:5b).

Although pondering Scripture is always significant, finding a pertinent passage that makes you tear up or takes your breath away is also beneficial. If we ponder our favorite pastor's Bible verse or the one on that cute t-shirt we just bought, that is wonderful. However, when it comes to making new tracks about who God says you are, taking time to search and pray for one that means something to *you* in your actual life is even better. This is especially beneficial for those of us who have grown up in the church and "had the gospel preached to us" (Hebrews 4:2a) but wondered where it's profited our actual lives. Patiently looking for a verse that the Spirit illuminates to us in a fresh, new way can help us see God's loving hand at work in the places and with the people that are important to us.

Lastly, after we ponder a pertinent verse, personalizing it helps me make new tracks too. When I use a degrading or disgusted tone with my husband (again) or judge the lady's outfit sitting in front of me at church, I'm learning to make new tracks. Instead of beating myself up and feeling guilty and ashamed, I'm learning to personalize Isaiah 43:4. Instead of just reading and memorizing Isaiah 43:4b, "Because you are precious and honored in my sight, and because I love you, I will give men in exchange for you and nations in place of your life," I picture Christ saying lovingly and tenderly to me, "Laura, you are precious and honored in my sight, and I love you." When I feel like I least deserve it, I am making new tracks by submitting and surrendering to a passage of Scripture. I am combining the gospel with faith, and in trying to trust the cross when I'm a hot mess, I am learning to lean into God's love and labels more often.

Although the Lord, in His love, may convict me about my tone, speech, and judgment, remember that conviction does not sound like a bully. It is not about beating myself up, but instead focusing on Christ's sacrifice and forgiveness. Personalizing and pondering pertinent passages about who God says I am *even and especially* when I mess up is helping me make new tracks of truth. Believing His Word more deeply when I'm a mess is moving Scripture from abstract to concrete beliefs, but it is also allowing me to hear conviction in love without getting defensive or self-abating. Learning to accept God's love and labels when we are at our ugliest gradually causes us to learn to receive correction with gratitude, which in turn helps us love others more deeply and permanently than punishing and condemning ourselves ever could.

Your Turn

This week, find a verse that speaks to your identity in Christ and write it below, starting with your name. Ponder and pray through it. Remember that Jesus knows your name. It is engraved in the palm of God's hand, yet we think it's weird to imagine or believe God would speak His Word directly to us (even though we have no problem picturing that for our daughter or BFF). When you mess up this week, picture Christ saying that verse to you. Does that verse feel more personal and meaningful? Journal anything you noticed below.

Remember to say it to yourself often and hear it as Jesus would say it to you. Hear it personally and tenderly like a mother would say to her daughter. If you are unable to hear it that way, keep asking the Holy Spirit for help. And remember 2 Corinthians 10:5b, which reminds us that making new tracks is not easy. Taking something, someone, or "every thought" captive requires strength and determination. However, by repeatedly submitting and surrendering to who Christ says we are in Scripture, we will move more quickly and joyfully into obedience and freedom.

Write your name here: _____ ,

Then write a verse that says who you are to Christ:

_____

_____

_____

_____

_____

_____

_____

FOR EXAMPLE

Nineteen

As I continued to pay attention to my ninety percent, I unearthed yet another significant lie that I had been believing most of my life about myself and my identity. I had always been embarrassed and ashamed of the brain God gave me. I have never been good at trivia or test-taking, and we've already discussed my hatred of all things related to numbers. Although I tell women in my speaking and writing, those I walk alongside in discipleship, and my friends and family that they are God's workmanship (Ephesians 2:10), complete in Him (Colossians 2:10), and reflect the Lord's glory (2 Corinthians 3:18a), and I believe it deeply for them, in my actual life I've never told my own family my ACT score.

Why? Because although the Lord has helped me learn to make new tracks and believe His love and labels for me more deeply, He still has more freedom for me. There are still areas in my life—and because God loves me, there will be more—where I fail to live out of the freedom Christ died to give me. However, as the Lord helps me personalize and ponder pertinent passages, He continues helping me make new tracks. Tracks that remind me that the nineteen I got on my ACT in 1988 does not prove I am dumb. It does not take away from my credibility as an author and speaker. Most of all, it does not change that I am still God's workmanship and reflect His glory.

Sometimes, a big part of making new tracks is not only replacing old condemning tracks with new ones. Sometimes, we have to physically and bravely step out into trusting who Christ says we are in order to believe deeper. Like Zacchaeus climbing out of the tree or Peter stepping out of the boat into the sea, sometimes we need to do *something*. Your something may not involve sharing your ACT score with thousands of women in a book you wrote, but perhaps you can pray about what it might look like to move toward living out of God's love and labels for you. What would it look like for you to pick up your mat and physically step into believing deeper?

C.S. Lewis put it this way: "Only a real risk tests the reality of a belief." As we learn to trust God more deeply, one of the ways to move beliefs deeper into our core is asking Him for the vision and courage to act out of His love and labels. If you are learning to enjoy God rather than finding your worth in your work or parenting, perhaps you can set aside ten minutes a day to simply sit in your backyard and be still. If, as you ask why, you are realizing that you want to be thanked and seen (like me), you could do something this week for someone completely anonymously. If, like me, you are struggling with wanting to be comfortable with the way you look, maybe you can skip wearing makeup to church on Sunday. If you wonder why God didn't make you smarter, ponder your pertinent passage and maybe practice saying "I don't know" without joking that you're dumb when you don't know where Belize is on a map.

There is freedom in laying at Jesus' feet the fears we have about the things we hate about ourselves but cannot seem to change. However, if we only pray or journal about these things, but we never do anything more with those fears than reflect on them, we risk failing to believe deeper. Testing the reality of the beliefs we are stepping into is not easy, but getting out of the boat will do more than merely thinking about believing deeper. It will be a risk that tests the reality of whether or not you are moving toward the freedom God has for you slowly, progressively, and in His loving protection.

Week Twelve

NOW REPEAT

"Punchinello laughed. 'Me, special? Why? I'm not very talented and my paint is peeling. Why do I matter to you?' Eli spoke very slowly. 'Because you're mine. That's why you matter to me.'"[26]
Max Lucado, in You Are Special

I wish a book could improve our ability to be and make disciples and help us believe deeper. I wish there was a formula to step into our identity in Christ more fully, or minimally abandon tracks in our minds that aren't in line with the truth of the gospel and easily create new paths that are. However, as far as I know, C.S. Lewis has the closest thing I can find to a silver bullet of faith: "Relying on God has to begin all over again every day as if nothing had yet been done." However, I would make one slight adjustment to Lewis' famous quote that admonishes us to remain connected to the Vine. In order for us to move what we know about God and His Word from abstractions in our mind to core beliefs we respond out of in our actual lives, we need to rely on God's *love* every day, and the best concrete way I've

[26] (Lucado, 1997)

been able to do that is by some of the tenets and practices to which you've just read and responded.

What we do and say in our actual lives, where we *really* are, helps us begin to expose the hidden thoughts and attitudes of the heart—thoughts and attitudes that are being transformed by the living and active Word of God and the resurrection power of Jesus Christ. Until we are able to expose the why of what we do and say in our actual lives, our relying on God and His love may be limited and rooted in striving. Additionally, when Christ's love and labels for us haven't become core beliefs we trust, we will likely be quick to judge others, demonize their motives, and fail to give them the benefit of the doubt because we do all of those things to ourselves. Moving to a place of knowing God and ourselves more deeply is not just about learning to submit and surrender to what Jesus says about us, but it is organically experiencing radical transformation in knowing and believing that everyone is known and loved by God. The more we accept and can receive His love and labels for us, the more readily and organically we will be able to accept them for others as well without striving or trying harder.

Paul talks about the crux of believing deeper in his letter to the Ephesians. He prays for them in the hope that they would "have power . . . to grasp how wide and long and high and deep is the love of Christ" (Ephesians 3:18b). God's love supersedes knowledge, and to be filled with that love is to be filled "to the measure of all the fullness of God" (Ephesians 3:19b). Why do we continue to pray, read Scripture, and pay attention to a deeper knowing of God and ourselves? Simply because we cannot exhaust or know completely the depth to which God loves us. He truly always has more for you, sister—more freedom and love. To believe in Him deeper and deeper is to be changed not only conceptually, but radically and repeatedly.

Star and Dot Stickers

Max Lucado wrote a thirteen-page board book titled *You Are Special* to illustrate what's taken me an entire response journal to try and articulate. In the book, wooden people called The Wemmicks give gold star stickers to talented, smart, and pretty Wemmicks and gray dot stickers to Wemmicks who are clumsy, tongue-tied, or get a nineteen on their ACT. When a gray-dotted fellow named Punchinello meets another Wemmick named Lucia, his imagination for life without any stickers blossomed. Lucia had somehow learned to come down the right side of the triangle. Because she only cared what Eli, the woodcarver who made the Wemmicks, thought of her, stickers of any shape or color did not stick to her. When Punchinello goes to see Eli to try and become like Lucia, Eli says Punchinello is special. Punchinello is confused as to why Eli thinks this since he has chipped paint and is devoid of gifts, but Eli encourages Punchinello to visit Eli every day so Eli can remind him how much he cares.

When Punchinello leaves Eli's workshop, he is still covered in the gray stickers the Wemmicks put on him in his less than enough-ness. He is not instantly morphed into a waxy wooden person devoid of stickers because Eli said he was special. As Punchinello leaves Eli's workshop, Eli says to him, "Remember . . . you are special because I made you. And I don't make mistakes," and then the little book ends with a beautiful glimpse into what happens when we start to lean in, even slightly, to God's love and labels where we really are: "Punchinello didn't stop, but in his heart he thought, *I think he really means it.* And when he did, a dot fell to the ground."[27]

Exposing doubt and stepping into deeper belief about God happens one dot at a time. As John Owen reminded us in Chapter One, change generally takes place "so slowly that it is not easily seen." However, one sticker is significant to those of us who've been trying to rid ourselves of the condemning opinions of ourselves and others.

---

[27] (Lucado, 1997)

One gray dot is more than we've ever been able to remove permanently, and even temporarily removing it comes with every inch of might and willpower we can muster.

John R. W. Stott wrote, "Faith's only function is to receive what grace offers"[28] (118). The process of moving toward the identity Christ has given us, toward greater obedience and deeper belief, is submitting and surrendering more and more, dot by dot, to the fact that God finds you wholly, completely, and utterly special because of the grace given to us at Calvary in and through Jesus Christ our Savior. It is as simple as returning to your Maker every day to be reminded to come down the right side of the triangle and, when you do, gradually watching your heart and your ninety percent become impervious to the opinions and labels of those around us, or even more pervasive to the critical opinions and labels we give ourselves.

Your Turn

Think about a time last week when you messed up. Maybe it was something monumental that impacted your marriage or severely fractured a relationship. Maybe it was something more mundane like an off-the-cuff remark or driving with road rage. Perhaps it was something in between like gossiping or being annoyed with someone because they were too gregarious or pretty.

Write a letter to yourself from your Maker regarding your mess-up. What would He say to you? What would He say about His love for you? Did He run toward you before you had a chance to apologize like the father did to the prodigal son in Luke 15? Does His finished work on the cross cover what you did? How is His tone? Did He use any smiley face emojis or hearts? Or was He stern or disappointed, trying to teach you a lesson? After you are done, compare what you wrote with Scripture passages like Luke 15:11-31, Psalms 103:8-12, Titus 3:4-5, and Romans 4:1-8. Does your perception of the Father's

---

[28] (Stott, 1994)

heart for you line up with what the Bible says? If not, do not worry! The Lord meets you where you are and in His great love always has more for us as we continue to believe deeper.

_____

_____

_____

_____

_____

_____

_____

_____

_____

_____

_____

_____

_____

_____

_____

_____

_____

_____

FOR EXAMPLE

Crying in Chicago

Three days before I had to have this manuscript to the publisher, I replaced an innocuous "For Example" story that I had originally written in Chapter Eleven with the one divulging my ACT score. After I made that edit, though, under the waterline of awareness, I had a pit in my stomach. I literally felt sick about admitting what I got on that cursed test. So, I started to ask myself, "Why?" Why did I feel naked and afraid sharing that number? Why did I keep thinking about whether or not I should omit that embarrassing example? I wanted to go down the right side of the triangle and trust that my identity wasn't in being smart or dumb, but in my actual life, I was nauseous.

The day before my book had to be to my publisher, I had to drive my daughter back to Purdue where she attends school. That meant I had seven hours in the car to ask why, and many things surfaced in that time of reflecting. I thought about the fact that in my first book, *Walking by the Homeless*, I had written about a traumatic childhood experience I endured. As I thought and prayed about that, I realized sharing that terrible and hurtful memory had been much easier than sharing my ACT score, which led me to ask why again. Why did sharing my score feel so awful and vulnerable? What was I afraid of?

Often, asking why reveals that we are afraid of something. The reason I wanted to be seen and thanked for things like taking pictures and volunteering was ultimately that I was afraid people did not think I was a good person who did good things. I was worried others would think my motives weren't genuine. The reason I often try to control and subtly manipulate my adult children's lives and relationships is because, under the waterline of awareness, I'm afraid they will endure hard things that might overwhelm them. The reason I am jealous of smart, beautiful women like Eileen Gu is that I am afraid I am not either of those things. Fear underlies most of our unintentional thoughts, habits, and actions. Therefore, when asking why exposes a fear I have, something I've learned to ask is "What is the worst thing that can happen if that fear comes true?"

As I drove past cornfields and windmills in Indiana, I wondered about that question. What was I afraid would be the impact of people reading my ACT score? It sounds like such a silly, petty question, but I've done this long enough to know that God meets me where I really am. Where I really was, was being deathly afraid to share my ACT score with the world. I was afraid people would wonder how I published a book with a score that low. I was afraid my readership or invitations to speak might decline. I was afraid someone would make fun of my score and intelligence on an Amazon review. Worst of all, I was afraid of what my children would think of me. I was afraid that my score would confirm to them that I wasn't that smart or that they would be embarrassed. Why was that my deepest fear?

I wasn't sure, but when I stopped for gas, I started listening to a sermon. Among several other things Pastor Judah Smith said that the Lord knew I needed to hear, he said, ". . . possessions and recognition and renown and accomplishments, that's not the stuff of life. The stuff of life is romance and love and connectivity with one another, but ultimately your connection with the Divine, and so he reaches and calls and he beckons, and he woos, and he dates and he romances you to call you unto himself, for this is where your home is and this is where you belong. You can't be defined by accomplishments and achievements and talents and abilities. You're defined by your eternal state and soul that was made in the image of God, that's who you are . . ."[29]

---

[29] (Churchome, 2022)

And as I continued driving through Chicago with tears flooding my eyes, I didn't stop. But in my heart, I thought, *I think he really means it.* And when I did, another dot fell to the ground.

Acknowledgements

Thanks to Mac McCarthy and Gravity Leadership for teaching me the practices in this book and for going and making disciples authentically and practically grounded in the grace and truth of Jesus Christ. Mac, you are true friend and brother in Christ. I'm so thankful for you and Josie.

Thank you to Emmie Nosek for your creative design work, your heart for women to know Jesus' love, and for your friendship. Thank you for all the time you spent reading emails and texts as we went back and forth on the cover art. I love how it turned out, and I love YOU!

Thank you to Leslee Baron, Jan Shackleton, and Grandpa-So-Much for your command of the English language (and its many confusing punctuation rules)! Your eye for details and the time you lovingly spent editing this book were an immense gift to me. I love you all!

Thank you to the many women I've walked alongside in discipleship. We have shared something sacred that will always bond us together. I love and cherish each of you, and thank you for never throwing anything at me when I reminded you (for the 800th time) to keep "Hugging Your Cactus!"

Thank you to my prayer team, Nilo, Leslee, Nicole, Kari, Chrissy, Kim, Jenny, Marlene, Patricia, Mary, Aimee, Cherl, Torey, Katie, and Renee. You know the past two years writing *Believe Deeper* were at times ugly and difficult for me. I am incredibly grateful and indebted to each of you for your steadfast prayers for my speaking and writing endeavors. I love you ladies.

Thank you to the team at Ten16 Press, and especially to Lauren Blue. As tired as I was of reading and editing my book, I have to think you were more so. Thank you for not just doing your job, but truly making me feel that you were as vested in making this book as clear, thought-provoking, and God-honoring as I was. You are a joy to work with, and I'm so thankful for you and Shannon.

Lastly, thank you to my husband Chris. You are my best friend, biggest cheerleader, and the love of my life. What a joy to publish this book in our thirtieth year of marriage. I love you so much, hon.

Bibliography

Breen, M. (2010). *Covenant and Kingdom: The DNA of the Bible.* Pawley Island, SC: 3DM.

Buchanan, M. (2006). *The Rest of God.* Nashville: W Publishing Group.

Call, M. (2019, August 8). Neuroplasticity: How to Use Your Brain's Malleability to Improve Your Well-being. Retrieved from: https://accelerate.uofuhealth.utah.edu/resilience/neuroplasticity-how-to-use-your-brain-s-malleability-to-improve-your-well-being.

Chandler, M. (2012). *Explicit Gospel.* Wheaton: Crossway.

Churchome. (2022, March 27). *You Need to Hurry | Judah Smith* [Video]. YouTube. Retrieved from: https://www.youtube.com/watch?v=5Mgdemga4uQ&t=105s.

Henri Nouwen Society. (1992). *"BEING THE BELOVED" (FULL SERMON Part 3) | Henri Nouwen, Hour of Power, Crystal Cathedral* [Video]. YouTube. Retrieved from: https://youtu.be/HCnhM-J2TP74.

John, N. S. (2014, December 8). Why Your Mind is Like an Iceberg. Retrieved from: https://www.huffpost.com/entry/why-your-mind-is-like-an-_b_6285584.

Keller, T. (2016). *Preaching.* New York, NY: Penguin Books.

Keller, T. (Accessed 2022, April 20). "Timothy J. Keller > Quotes > Quotable Quote." Goodreads. Retrieved from: https://www.goodreads.com/quotes/224484-a-faith-without-some-doubts-is-like-a-human-body.

Ladd, G. E. (1993). *A Theology of the New Testament.* Grand Rapids: Eerdmans Publishing.

Lucado, M. (1997). *You Are Special.* Wheaton: Crossway.

Luther, M. (2011). *Martin Luther's Commentary on Galatians.* Coppell: ReadaClassic.com.

McGrath, A. (1994). *Christian Theology: An Introduction.* Cambridge: Blackwell.

Merriam-Webster. (2022, Apr 1). "Condemn" Retrieved from: https://www.merriam-webster.com/dictionary/condemn.

Press, O. U. (nd). *Oxford Advanced Learner's Dictionaries.* Retrieved from: https://www.oxfordlearnersdictionaries.com/definition/english/reflect.

Reinke, T. (2015). *Newton on the Christian Life.* Wheaton: Crossway.

Sternke, B., & Tebbe, M. (2016, April 21). How Covenant and Calling Work. Retrieved from: https://www.gravityleadership.com/discipleship-training/good-news/covenant-calling-work/.

Sternke, B., & Tebbe, M. (2016, March 24). How to Start Repenting: DIG. Retrieved from: https://www.gravityleadership.com/discipleship-training/discerning-kingdom/dig.

Sternke, B., & Tebbe, M. (2016, March 24). The Ways Against Love. Retrieved from: https://gravityleadership.com/discipleship-training/bad-news/ways-against-love/.

Stott, J. R. (1994). *The Message of Romans.* Downer's Grove: Inter-Varsity Press.

Strobel, L. (2000). *The Case for Faith.* Grand Rapids, MI: Zondervan.

The NIV Study Bible. (1984). Grand Rapids, MI: Zondervan.

© Laura Sandretti

ABOUT THE AUTHOR

Laura Sandretti is a Christian speaker, author, and blogger. She is also a former high school teacher and ministry director and has her master's degree in Theological Studies from Trinity Evangelical Divinity School. Laura has been married to her husband, Chris, for thirty years, and they have three adult biological children, Hannah, Casey, and Faithe, and Polo, who has been part of their family for almost ten years. Laura enjoys volunteering, cycling, and praying daily for grandchildren.

Believe Deeper is Laura's third book. To find out more about Laura and her ministry, please visit www.laurasandretti.com.

CPSIA information can be obtained
at www.ICGtesting.com
Printed in the USA
JSHW050808210722
28310JS00005B/11